MW01205431

INCONVENIENT **FAITH**

A GOSPEL-ROOTED DIALOGUE WITH NEW ATHEISM

Travis J. Bond

Adapted from a Thesis-Project Approved by
GORDON-CONWELL THEOLOGICAL SEMINARY

For the Degree
DOCTOR OF MINISTRY
January 2017

Inconvenient Faith
A Gospel-Rooted Dialogue with New Atheism

First Printing: January 2017

ISBN: 978-1-365-64035-3

Lulu Press
http://www.lulu.com

Printed in the United States of America

Cover photo courtesy of *Robert Umenhofer Photography*
www.robertumenhofer.com

For Sarah.
A constant reminder to me that there is a God.
And He is good.

You never really understand a person until you consider things from his point of view – until you climb into his skin and walk around in it.

- Atticus Finch,
from Harper Lee's novel *To Kill a Mockingbird*

TABLE OF CONTENTS

LIST OF FIGURES

In 2010, a televised report from ABC News caught my attention: "Atheist Ministers Struggle with Leading the Faithful." Over the years I have battled all variety of diverse and sundry temptations common to man. This particular one, however – outright and sustained disbelief in a personal God *while serving* in pastoral ministry – is foreign to me. And intriguing. Having served my first eight years of full-time ministry in Baptist saturated South Carolina and Roman Catholic drenched Pittsburgh, pure atheism was simply not an often encountered perspective.

Subsequent to those first eight years of ministry, I have now spent an additional six years in blue-state, hyper-educated, increasingly non-religious Massachusetts. Since that 2010 report on atheist clergy first aired, I have become more attuned to both the growing skepticism within American culture generally, as well as an accompanying hostility toward evangelical Christianity specifically. Following the Bush administration's overt evangelicalism, Bible-based Christianity appears to have moved in the last fifteen years beyond the margins of mere dismissal – or even acceptability.

A historical and orthodox view of Scripture is increasingly categorized by unbelievers today as not just irrelevant to the contemporary world, but downright *hostile* to human flourishing. The following study seeks to better understand what role the new, militant atheism plays in this cultural shift. By God's grace, the pages ahead will help identify a real and present danger to Christian discipleship while simultaneously preparing a path forward to graciously answer the atheist's charge.

ACKNOWLEDGEMENTS

Saint Augustine once asked then answered, "What does love look like? It has the hands to help others." If this is true, then I am blessed with the love of many for I surely have experienced the helping hands of many. First, I am thankful to my Savior who saw fit to bestow enough ability – limited as it may be – to allow completion of this project.

Medway Community Church has been my family for over six years, proving themselves time and again to be a gracious, giving, Gospel-loving gathering of saints. I am so thankful for these brothers and sisters in Christ who completed my surveys, listened to my sermons, supported my studies, and provided a sabbatical to complete this thesis. The MCC staff is excellent, and each of my colleagues picked up additional duties to allow my time away. The Board of Elders – a band of brothers – promised upon my initial employment in 2010 that, when the time was right, they would support doctoral studies. Their word was gold.

I am grateful for those who have taught me at Gordon-Conwell, particularly David Currie, Ken Swetland, and my academic advisor Gordy Isaac. A special thanks as well to Chris Gooley, who volunteered his time and expertise for statistical analysis, and Courtney Tierney who typed a LOT of notes. And many thanks to my daughters, who sacrificed much Daddy-time over the years to allow completion of these studies.

More than anyone, though, I am grateful for Sarah, the bride of my youth and the joy of my heart. She spent countless hours reading, re-reading, editing, then re-editing yet again. Her support is unflagging. Her godliness unmatched. Her wisdom and beauty a gift I do not deserve.

Introduction

Objective, absolute truth has fallen on hard times. Although it largely did away with a personal God, the enlightenment (mid 1600's to late 1700's), which paved the way to modernity (early 1800's to late 1900's), assumed at least the existence of truth. Philosophical conceptions like good and evil, the assumption of right and wrong – together with moral absolutes, these abstractions were widely considered throughout modernity to be a given. However, brewing beneath these historical eras, in the shadows, was a competing hypothesis that if there exists no personal God perhaps there also exists no ground for absolute truth. This idea, commonly known as relativism, has captured the church's attention for over four decades.

Section 1 of 5
History: Relativistic Roots

Relativism is the concept that points of view have no absolute truth or validity but only relative, subjective value. Subjective value is dependent on differing vantage points and perception. This line of thought, once followed, eventually demands that knowledge, truth, and morality can only exist in relation to other things. None of these items will be trans-cultural, trans-generational, or absolute.

Pontius Pilate, widely regarded as one of the most craven figures in all of human history, could be considered an ahead-of-his time, ancient-world relativist.

> Then Pilate said to him, 'So you are a king?' Jesus answered, 'You say that I am a king. For this purpose I was born and for this purpose I have come into the world—to bear witness to the truth. Everyone who is of the truth listens to my voice.' Pilate said to him, 'What is truth?' (John 18:37-38a)[1]

Pilate's cowardice – observing Christ's innocence yet condemning Jesus nonetheless – was not a mere character flaw. Rather, his weakness was birthed from a worldview in which the concept of absolute truth was not something to be admired, but rather disdained. A belief of shifting morality then, having germinated and taken root, will naturally bear the fruit of relativism.

Although Pilate will be the most recognizable of the relativistic forerunners, his was not an anomalous view. Arcesilaus, 300 years before Christ, believed that "our understanding is not capable of knowing what truth is." Carneades (200 B.C.) said we can never comprehend truth. Gorgias, born 485 B.C. stated, "What is right but what we prove to be right? And what is truth but what we believe to be truth?"[2] Relativism, then, is not new. Its cultural offspring however, postmodernism, is. Postmodernism was a late 20th century movement – catalyzed by the sexual revolution as much as anything else – characterized by skepticism, subjectivism, and relativism; it is a general suspicion of reason. Put simply, postmodernism may be thought of as relativism gone mainstream.

Postmodern Pivot

For the past four decades, postmodernism has been the source of much angst within the evangelical subculture. Reasons for anxiety are fairly straightforward: the Christian framework rests on the concept that

---

[1] Unless otherwise indicated, all Scripture references taken from the English Standard Version (ESV), Wheaton, IL: Crossway Bibles, a publishing ministry of Good News Publishers, 2001.

[2] Maureen Carter, "What is Truth?," accessed March 14, 2015, http://www.whatistruth.org.uk/whatistruth.php.

truth is trans-cultural, is trans-generational, and can be known. The recipient of Pilate's scornful "what is truth?" question – the God-man standing before Pilate – is understood by evangelicals to be the very embodiment of truth. He is "the way, the truth and the life." (John 14:6)

As postmodernism gained traction through the 1970's and 80's it took the American church some time to realize what was happening and ultimately accept the need to pivot from a once effective approach that presumed a common definition for truth. Everything from Sunday worship to informal outreach endeavors to evangelistic programs have been forced to re-think what it means to contextualize in a culture that does not accept the existence of a ground for knowable truth. Instead, the late twentieth and early twenty-first century American will typically claim to most value authenticity, vulnerability, and the experiential. Propositional truth as a presupposition has quickly become a value of the past.

One unplanned and unexpected side-benefit of the postmodern ethos did arise, however. If all religious propositions are understood to be on equal footing, Christianity at least received a place at the table. Christians in general, including Bible-believing evangelicals, have been culturally welcome more or less to bring along their paraphernalia and erect a tent in the marketplace of ideas, alongside all the other tents. "To the unknown God" – one statue among all the other statues, as it were. That environment however – one where a *Christian* ethic was not the majority but was at least part of the plurality – is quickly being swept away, replaced by something noticeably more hostile to the Judeo-Christian ethic.

A New Era Dawns

In the summer of 2014, the Ice Bucket Challenge, a fundraising initiative for Amyotrophic Lateral Sclerosis (ALS, also known as Lou Gehrig's Disease), raised awareness for the disease, across the nation, via social networking. Of special note in the medical community is that those diagnosed with ALS earlier in life tend to live much longer on average than those diagnosed later on. In the case of the most famous ALS victim alive today, Dr. Stephen Hawking, doctors surmise that this progressive neurodegenerative disease has essentially, after 50 years, run its course and burnt itself out.[3]

---

[3] "Stephen Hawking's ALS Appears to Have 'almost burnt out', Says Neurologist," accessed April 16, 2015, http://www.sciencerecorder.com/news/stephen-hawkings-als-appears-to-have-almost-burnt-out-says-neurologist/.

For the current presentation then, the idea is a simple one: *postmodernism is the Lou Gehrig's disease of cultural thought, now beginning the process of burning itself out.* Postmodernism has run its course and the cultural damage left in its wake is profound, yet postmodernism with its core value of "tolerance" was not a movement seeking to eradicate Christianity. Rather, *what has become known as "the New Atheism" a brash, militant brand of agnostic thought, is today sweeping in to fill the vacuum postmodernism leaves behind.* This worldview creates a clear and present need for a coherent, evangelical, response.

An atheist is a philosophical materialist who believes there exists nothing beyond the natural, physical world – no supernatural creative intelligence behind the observable universe. An atheist believes there is no soul that outlasts the body nor any miracles except in the sense of natural phenomena that remain to be understood.[4] Similar to a recognition of postmodernism rooted in the ancient relativists, one can identify many of the roots for today's foremost atheists. The early twentieth century, within the Russian Revolution of 1917, saw the rise of the first explicitly atheistic state.[5] Likewise, men like Isaac Asimov, Sigmund Freud, and Bertrand Russell made no doubt of their overt skepticism. Nevertheless, in bygone eras there was a common tone related to the loss of belief in a personal God. Al Mohler suggests, "one of the most notable hallmarks of this Victorian loss of faith is a sense of mourning... it is conspicuously lacking in the New Atheism... no sense that something precious is now gone. Instead, there is actually a sense of celebration that theism is finally left behind."[6]

Seth Andrews, a once vocal Christian and radio-personality, has made no secret of his belief that atheism *remains* culturally unacceptable. As recently as 2013, he stated with no small flair for the dramatic, "Announcing you're an atheist is like dipping yourself in jet fuel and showing up for a candlelight church service. The crowd is convinced you're going up in flames, and they're terrified that you'll take others with you."[7] Despite the creative imagery, Andrews' implication that atheism is a near persecuted class bears little accord with the facts. Recent polls suggest

---

[4] Richard Dawkins, *The God Delusion* (Boston: Houghton Mifflin Company, 2008), 35.

[5] R. Albert Mohler, Jr., *Atheism REMIX: A Christian Confronts the New Atheists* (Wheaton, IL: Crossway Books, 2008), 27.

[6] Mohler, *REMIX*, 25.

[7] Seth Andrews, *Deconverted: A Journey from Religion to Reason* (Denver, CO: Outskirts Press, 2013), ii.

that "non-religion" is the fastest growing religious identification in the United States. College students in America are today the least religious demographic in the nation.[8]

Released in March of 2015, the General Social Survey conducted by the University of Chicago found that the number of Americans leaving organized religion has reached a new high at 21 percent. Also in 2015, the Barna Group released a 2015 study revealing that 1 in 4 unchurched adults in the country now self-identify as atheist or agnostic.[9] The conclusion to be drawn from such polls is a simple one: atheism today is more widely accepted than ever before in our nation's history. When atheists speak, millions are now listening.

Section 2 of 5
Commonality: The Presupposition of Truth

It was only after the Enlightenment that atheism progressed into any sort of real, intellectual force.[10] In the Western World however, relativistic thought and the postmodern movement continued until recently to receive most of the press. Beginning with the 21st century however, what is commonly called the New Atheism arose – a brazen, unyielding brand of atheistic ideology that has successfully altered the philosophical landscape. At the forefront of this movement has been the self-dubbed "four-horsemen of the non-Apocalypse": Richard Dawkins, Christopher Hitchens (now deceased), Sam Harris, and Daniel Dennett. Each of these men, to a striking degree, has helped set the agenda for a cultural dialogue and embrace of atheistic doctrine. Of special note then is that to varying degrees each of these men, and those they have influenced, have increasingly cast aside the framework of postmodernism.

---

[8] Dan Barker, *Godless: How an Evangelical Preacher Became One of America's Leading Atheists* (Ulysses Press: Berkeley, CA, 2008), xv.

[9] Stoyan Zaimov, "1 in 4 Americans Don't Believe in God; Lack of Trust in Local Churches Cited as a Reason Why Adults Are Leaving the Faith," accessed March 26, 2015, http://m.christianpost.com/news/barnas-2015-state-of-atheism-report-finds-one-in-four-americans-dont-believe-god-exists--136327/

[10] Mohler, *REMIX*, 18.

Rejecting Relativism

Having spent the past forty years in a cultural milieu that rejects "simplistic", Judeo-Christian notions of right and wrong, the Christian will find it somewhat jarring to discover philosophical agreement within a camp so adamantly opposed to evangelical presuppositions. Nevertheless, a common thread among the New Atheists is their rejection of the relativistic framework in favor of, to the Christian, far more familiar language. "We agree," says Harris, "that if one of us is right, the other is wrong. The Bible is either the word of God, or it isn't. Either Jesus offers humanity the one, true path to salvation...or he does not."[11] Dawkins agrees: "When two opposite points of view are expressed with equal force, the truth does not necessarily lie midway between them. It is possible for one side to be simply wrong."[12] Dennett even reacts with disdain to a Jewish clergyman possessing postmodern sensibilities. "David Wolpe said, 'Even though the stories of the Torah may not be true, the Torah is true.' What does that mean? I don't know what that means. Something is either true or it's not true. Something is either factual or it's not factual... it's a childish thing to tell people in the 21st century."

In this hunger for intellectual rationalism, the New Atheism has consciously chosen to marry itself to scientific naturalism. Hard-wired, as it were, to its own concept of scientific knowledge, modern day atheism has become in many ways a refutation of the postmodern mood. The New Atheists are not relativistic, and they do not accept that all truth is merely the product of social construction.[13] In fact, "to lose the conviction that you can actually be right about anything," says Harris, "seems a recipe for the End of Days chaos... I believe that relativism and pragmatism have already done much to muddle our thinking on a variety of subjects, many of which have more than a passing relevance to the survival of civilization."[14]

Embracing the Rational

If there is one sphere in which the atheist most prides himself upon, it is the embrace of eminently rationalistic thought patterns. Much is made, for instance, even of the requirement for a term like "atheism." No one ever identifies oneself as a non-astrologer, or a non-alchemist, so what

---

[11] Sam Harris, *Letter to a Christian Nation* (New York: Vintage Books, 2008), 3.
[12] Dawkins, *Delusion*, 19.
[13] Mohler, *REMIX*, 88.
[14] Harris, *Letter*, 180.

need exists, the atheist asks, to label reasonable people who object to unjustified religious beliefs?[15]   Such rationalistic delight takes on a noticeable scorn when directed toward intelligentsia who possess a relativistic bent. Says Harris:

> Many intellectuals...place all worldviews more or less on an equal footing. No one is ever really right about what he believes; he can only point to a community of peers who believe likewise. Suicide bombing isn't really wrong, in any absolute sense, it just seems so from the Parochial perspective of Western Culture... convictions of this sort generally go by the name of "relativism," and they seem to offer a rationale for not saying anything too critical about the beliefs of others. But most forms of relativism – including moral relativism, which seems especially well subscribed – are nonsensical.[16]

The same type of ridicule evidenced above, however, is certainly not reserved for the postmodern alone. It is ultimately unleashed upon the Christian ethic with more than equal ferocity.   When responding, for example, to the suggestion that national leadership will function best when resting upon an immutable ground of truth, Dan Barker bites back:

> How does truth fare in the "theistic universe" where the despot is named Jehovah? The God of Scripture slaughtered entire groups of people that offended his vanity. "Happy shall be he that taketh and dasheth thy little ones against the stones," he advised (Psalm 137:9), threatening those with the wrong religion that "their women with child shall be ripped up" (Hosea 13:16). He also sent bears to attack 42 children who teased a prophet (II Kings 2:23-24), punished innocent offspring to the fourth generation (Exodus 20:5), discriminated against the handicapped (Leviticus 21:18-23) and promised that fathers and sons would eat each other (Ezekiel 5:10), among other actions that we would find repugnant in a human being. In this theistic universe, morality is severed from reality and reduced to flattering the Sovereign.[17]

---

[15] Harris, *Letter*, 51.
[16] Harris, *Letter*, 178.
[17] Barker, *Godless*, 217.

It should be noted that although the New Atheist self-consciously clings to a surprisingly traditional view of knowable truth, this conviction does not necessarily burrow itself into an understanding of ethics or human morality. It appears the supposition that objective truth allows one to declare right from wrong can be quite useful when setting crosshairs upon either a liberal relativist or a conservative Christian. A belief in objective truth becomes inconvenient however, should one's *personal* biases fall outside the margin of social conservatism.

Contemporary atheists have almost a universally high regard for science. Most atheists possess a belief in the universal applicability of the scientific method, together with the conviction that empirical science constitutes the most authoritative worldview – even to the exclusion of other viewpoints.[18] This conviction however, when applied to certain hot-button social issues, can create points of tension. For example, given the weight of scientific evidence, little argument is now offered against the proposition that human embryos are indeed examples of human life. Therefore, by absolutist religious convictions, abortion would simply be wrong given its termination of life. Yet our atheist neighbors will disagree.

Richard Dawkins offers an alternative to the absolutist view of truth once it is applied within the social sphere: "A consequentialist or utilitarian is likely to approach the abortion question in a very different way, by trying to weigh up suffering. Does the embryo suffer?... Does the pregnant woman, or her family, suffer if she does not have an abortion?"[19] The reader will note how the question of morality begins to shift, then. It's no longer *merely* a question of truth – right or wrong. It's a question of shifting truth when *applied* to the human experience.

Section 3 of 5
Disagreement: The Ground for Morality

New Atheism is deeply concerned to show that morality need not, indeed does not, find its grounding in any sort of religious superstructure.

---

[18] Austin Hughes, "The Folly of Scientism," accessed April 17, 2015, http://www.thenewatlantis.com /publications/the-folly-of-scientism.

[19] Dawkins, *Delusion*, 331.

This appears to be in reaction to a charge frequently levied against atheism from the religious sphere – the necessity of deity for the grounding of morality. Our atheist friends sharply disagree with such grounding.

The Origin of Atheistic Morality

Within New Atheism, there does not appear to be agreement for the *source* of morality, only unanimity that the source is not religion. Sam Harris, bringing a doctoral degree in neuroscience, seeks a purely naturalistic answer: "There will probably come a time when we achieve a detailed understanding of human happiness and of ethical judgments themselves, at the level of the brain."[20] Dawkins is not entirely sure of morality's origin, but confident we need not consult the Scriptures:

> No religious leader today (apart from the likes of the Taliban or the American Christian equivalent) thinks like Moses. But that is my whole point. All I am establishing is that modern morality, wherever else it comes from, does not come from the Bible... How, then, do we decide what is right and what is wrong? No matter how we answer that question, there is a consensus about what we do as a matter of fact consider right and wrong: a consensus that prevails surprisingly widely. The consensus has no obvious connection with religion.[21]

Christopher Hitchens is also representative of this belief when he asserts, "the awareness of the difference between right and wrong is innate in human beings."[22] And yet, a reasonable hesitation exists before embracing this notion of wide consensus regarding morality. Even a casual familiarity with sociology will reveal that grounding human morality in nothing more than human solidarity has canyon sized gaps. Humans possess competing instincts and often a corresponding inability to choose between those two instincts.[23] Minister-turned-atheist Dan Barker, in an attempted swipe against theism, actually does the innate morality argument a disservice:

> There is no "universal moral urge" and not all ethical systems agree. Polygamy, human sacrifice, infanticide, cannibalism

---

[20] Sam Harris, *The End of Faith: Religion, Terror, and the Future of Reason* (New York: W.W. Norton & Company Inc, 2004), 175.

[21] Dawkins, *Delusion*, 297-298.

[22] Darren Doane, "Collision," accessed on April 11, 2015 https://www.youtube.com/watch?v =cCUmKP4NFKs.

[23] Doane, "Collision."

(Eucharist), wife beating, self-mutilation, foot binding, preemptive war, torture of prisoners, circumcision, female genital mutilation, racism, sexism, punitive amputation, castration and incest are perfectly "moral" in certain cultures. Is god confused?[24]

If human morality and the distinction of good and evil is not to be grounded in a universal law-giver, than where might such standards find root? Beyond the hoped-for-perhaps-one-day-discovery at the level of neurobiology, atheists posit ethical grounding either in nature (generally) or Darwinian natural selection (specifically). The "mistake" or "by-product" hypothesis is one in which natural selection, beginning in ancestral times, programmed into the human brain altruistic urges right alongside sexual urges and hunger urges and so on. Kindness, it is theorized, was worked out in the context of small, nomadic bands of kin who would function as potential reciprocators for generosity, empathy, and pity. Contemporary society no longer self-limits altruism to small tribes of course, but courtesy of natural selection the altruistic urges yet remain.

It is just like sexual desire. We can no more help ourselves feeling pity when we see a weeping unfortunate (who is unfeeling and unable to reciprocate) than we can help ourselves feeling lust for a member of the opposite sex (who may be infertile or otherwise unable to reproduce). Both are misfiring, Darwinian mistakes: blessed, precious mistakes. Do not for one moment, think of such Darwinizing as demeaning or reductive of the noble emotions of compassion and generosity.[25]

One wonders in the schema above on what basis the urges to kindness or empathy matter at all. Absent a universal law-giver for instance, upon whose standard might empathy be labeled "noble?" The atheist answer is not to root morality in a supernatural origin of goodness, or humanity as image-bearers of God, but rather to see a universal moral grounding in the calculus of happiness versus suffering.

The Criteria for Atheistic Morality

In reading the New Atheist literature, one is encouraged to walk away with the impression that Christianity's search for universal moral propositions is energy unnecessarily spent. "Although a few extreme ethical dilemmas might arise in one's lifetime," Barker suggests, "basic

---

[24] Barker, *Godless*, 113.
[25] Dawkins, *Delusion*, 253.

day-to-day morality is a simple matter of kindness, respect and reason. Once I shed the religio-psychological frame of mind, I learned that the Christian 'struggle' with morality is overblown."[26] Harris believes a rational approach to ethics will become possible once it is understood that questions of right and wrong are simply questions about the happiness and suffering of sentient creatures.[27]   And 'Carl,' a closeted atheist Lutheran pastor states with no small lack of originality, "More and more, I think Christianity has to do with living a good life. I think the lessons of Jesus are profound and apply to life, without needing any sense of 'other'."[28]

Religious skeptics have little interest in seeking out clergy to assist with their moral decision-making.   Vehemently opposing the label "a-moral," the skeptic will turn to moral philosophers as the real professionals when it comes to distinguishing right from wrong.[29] With the philosopher's assistance then, and the use of one's own rationalistic and naturalistic methodology, the atheist seeks to be happy, balanced, moral, and intellectually fulfilled.[30]

The stubborn brick-wall to all this, however, is the nagging reality that happiness for the one does not always equal happiness for the other. In fact, one individual's happiness might quite often *require* another individual's suffering.   So on what basis may such distinctions be prioritized? For the clearest example of competing desires, one need only return to the previously discussed topic of pregnancy termination. Here, few atheists – anchored as they are in the elevation of scientific naturalism – will argue that "life" is not a reasonable description of the pre-born. And yet, the identification of human life seems to matter very little in the actual analysis.

> *Embryology confirms morality. The words "unborn child," even when used in a politicized manner, describe a material reality. However this only opens the argument rather than closes it. There may be many circumstances in which it is not desirable to carry a fetus to full term… it is probably less miserable an outcome than the vast number of deformed or idiot children who would otherwise have been born, or stillborn, or whose brief lives would have been a*

---

[26] Barker, Godless, 210.

[27] Harris, *End*, 281.

[28] Daniel C. Dennett and Linda Lascola, *Caught in the Pulpit: Leaving Belief Behind* (United States of America, 2013), 36.

[29] Dawkins, *Delusion*, 265.

[30] Dawkins, *Delusion*, 23.

torment to themselves and others... All thinking people recognize a painful conflict of rights and interests in this question, and strive to achieve a balance. The only proposition that is completely useless, either morally or practically, is the wild statement that sperms and eggs are all potential lives...and must be protected by law.[31]

So it appears a guiding principle of atheistic morality is that one must first determine what causes harm – and just avoid that.[32] Harris confidently asserts, in a debate with evangelical pastor Rick Warren, "I'm not at all a moral relativist. I think it's quite common among religious people to believe that atheism entails moral relativism. I think there is an absolute right and wrong." Time and time again, however, to be convinced that evil is actually evil – in an objective sense – the atheist must borrow from an objective moral framework to support his point.[33] Phrased differently, atheists must steal standards from the Christian faith in order to make their very argument. They desire to "climb into the Christian car and drive it into a tree, yet the atheist does not have any car of his own.[34]

The Superiority of Atheistic Morality

It is important to recognize that when taken in total, the aim of atheistic moral arguments are not merely intended to divorce objective ethical definitions from a personal God or universal law giver. Rather, the argumentation is rather clearly directed toward the end goal of asserting atheistic morality's superiority and religious morality's inferiority – even wickedness. To their credit, the New Atheists are equal opportunity offenders here, displaying unveiled scorn for all three of the world's major religions (Christianity, Islam, Judaism). "The preferred source of absolute morality," says Dawkins, "is usually a holy book of some kind, interpreted as having an authority far beyond its history's capacity to justify."[35]

The Christian Bible is one filled with a variety of styles from a variety of authors which both believing and unbelieving theologians have long recognized should be read within their unique genre and redemptive context. The New Atheists are more interested, however, in flattening the

---

[31] Christopher Hitchens, *God is not Great: How Religion Poisons Everything* (New York: Hatchette Book Group, 2009), 221.

[32] Barker, *Godless*, 214.

[33] Ravi Zacharias, *The End of Reason: A Response to the New Atheists* (Grand Rapids, MI: Zondervan, 2008), 52.

[34] Doane, "Collision".

[35] Dawkins, *Delusion*, 267.

Biblical landscape and interpreting virtually everything on paper in light of a 21st century chronological arrogance. "The Bible may, indeed does, contain a warrant for trafficking in humans, for ethnic cleansing, for slavery, for bride-price, and for indiscriminate massacre, but we are not bound by any of it because it was put together by crude, uncultured human mammals."[36] Dawkins agrees, asserting that the Bible's story of Joshua's destruction of Jericho, and the promised land invasion narrative in general, is "morally indistinguishable" from Hitler's invasion of Poland or Hussein's massacre of the Kurds.[37] Barker insures that without ignoring Old Testament atrocities, the New Testament is not left unimpeached: "Any ideology that makes its point by threatening violence is morally bankrupt. Hitler's horrible ovens, at least, were relatively quick. The torment Jesus promised is a 'fire that shall never be quenched.' Anyone who believes in hell is at heart not moral at all."[38]

In addition to a dubious exegetical process when interacting directly with Holy Scripture, the New Atheists are eager to attack Christian morality on three additional fronts as well. First, they are quick to point out the dissonance between Scriptural precept and Christian obedience – an easy accusation to make, quite frankly. Second, they are eager to highlight a patronizing tone among the professing evangelicals: "When I interacted with my parents, I couldn't help but hear that nauseating tone of pity and condescension that so often oozes from the mouths of the morally superior."[39] Third, the New Atheists argue that not only is Scriptural morality deeply flawed, but it simultaneously diverts time and energy from the "real" moral problems of the world. Harris states:

> One of the most pernicious effects of religion is that it tends to divorce morality from the reality of human and animal suffering. Religion allows people to imagine that their concerns are moral when they are not – that is, when they have nothing to do with suffering or its alleviation. This explains why Christians like yourself expend more "moral" energy opposing abortion than fighting genocide. It explains why you are more concerned about human embryos than about the lifesaving promise of stem-cell research.

---

[36] Hitchens. *Great,* 102.
[37] Dawkins, *Delusion*, 280.
[38] Barker, *Godless*, 220-221.
[39] Andrews, *Deconverted*, 118.

29

And it explains why you can preach against condom use in sub-Saharan Africa while millions die from AIDS there each year.[40]

Once the inferiority of Christian morality has been established, the table is then set for the New Atheists' most jarring attack. To continue to hold to such an antiquated system, the atheist argues – in the now enlightened 21st century – requires an ignorance and/or stupidity of profound proportions.

Section 4 of 5
Dismissal: the 'Absurdity' of Faith

Mark Twain once stated that "heaven is for climate, hell for society." This passing, dismissive, and somewhat amused view of religion was once prominent amongst western atheism. Yet the tide has turned. If New Atheism seeks the eradication of Christianity in a way that postmodernism never did, a chief methodology of attack is to levy the charge that religious faith is both intellectually untenable and altogether embarrassing.

Belief is Uneducated and Adolescent

Although men and women of faith, particularly evangelical faith, are scattered throughout American universities and corporations, the New Atheism is aggressive in its charge that people of faith are, for good reason, under-represented in positions of influence. "The nineteenth century is the last time," Dawkins believes, "when it was possible for an educated person to admit to believing in miracles like the virgin birth without embarrassment. When pressed, many educated Christians today are too loyal to deny the virgin birth and the resurrection. But it embarrasses them because their rational minds know it is absurd."[41] Elsewhere he adds, "Great scientists who profess religion...stand out for their rarity and are a subject of amused bafflement to their peers in the academic community."[42]

Chronological arrogance, the assertion that contemporary intellectualism is superior to days gone by, is often front and center in the attack upon religion. Hitchens believes, "One must state it plainly. Religion

---

[40] Harris, *Letter*, 25.
[41] Dawkins, *Delusion*, 187.
[42] Dawkins, *Delusion*, 125.

comes from the period of human prehistory where nobody...had the smallest idea what was going on. It comes from the bawling and fearful infancy of our species, and is a babyish attempt to meet our inescapable demand for knowledge."[43] Harris gets in on the game as well, "Imagine that we could revive a well-educated Christian of the fourteenth century. The man would prove to be a total ignoramus, except on matters of faith... There are two explanations for this: either we perfected our religious understanding of the world a millennium ago...or religion, being the mere maintenance of dogma, is one area of disclosure that does not admit of progress."[44]

New Atheism is hungry for society to move past the adolescence of religious faith to the freedom that divorce from deity permits. Given this desire, there exists a concerted effort to establish sociological progress as a launching pad for the abolition of faith. Dennett states:

> *The transparency of information engendered by electronic media has dramatically changed the epistemological environment – the environment of knowledge, belief, error, illusion, confidence – that we all inhabit. It threatens the security and stability of all institutions that depend on confidence and trust – which includes religion ... Religion has changed more in the last century than in the previous millennium, and I predict that it will change more in the next twenty years than it did in the last century, for just this reason. The old ways, the traditional ways, no longer work in the new world of universal transparency.*[45]

Finally, having addressed Christianity's under-representation in the intelligentsia, the superiority of the modern age, and the acceleration of progress, New Atheists offer their final charge against theism's intellectual tenability: it's just stupid. Harris asserts, "Among developed nations, American stands alone in these convictions. Our country now appears, as at no other time her history, like a lumbering, bellicose, dim-witted giant... the combination of great power and great stupidity is simply terrifying."[46]

Barker, when reviewing creationism and intelligent design, adds to the charge for idiocy, "People who are impressed with the design argument are like the guy who is amazed at all the rivers that were made to flow along

---

43 Hitchens, *Great*, 64.
44 Harris, *End*, 42.
45 Dennett, *Caught*, 73-74.
46 Harris, *Letter*, xi.

state borders... this is backward, hindsight design – our minds imposing a pattern after the fact."[47] And Andrews reflects on the evangelical ethos, "Ignorance is celebrated. Curiosity is quelled. Fear is cultivated. Science is largely distrusted. And brainwashed individuals struggle to make sense of their own lives as they frantically struggle to pound the square peg of religion into the round hole of reason."[48]

Religion is Delusional and Irrational

Accusations against a Christian's cerebral reliability are admittedly insulting, but not terribly new or troubling. However, the 21st century atheist increasingly moves beyond accusations of mere foolishness or lack of education to ascribe actual deranged thinking. Barker recounts that within his transition away from fundamentalist Christianity, he became convinced the Bible offers no reliable source of truth, but instead is "unscientific, irrational, contradictory, absurd, unhistorical, uninspiring and morally unsatisfying."[49] For others, the process of demythologizing Scripture became both "exciting and troubling" as it increasingly reveals belief in Scripture's historicity to be utterly ridiculous.[50]

Dawkins characteristically pulls no punches, setting forward his views unveiled: "When one person suffers from a delusion, it is called insanity. When many people suffer from a delusion, it is called Religion."[51] Harris agrees:

> We have names for people who have many beliefs for which there is no rational justification. When their beliefs are extremely common we call them 'religious'; otherwise, they are likely to be called 'mad', 'psychotic' or 'delusional'...And so, while religious people are not generally mad, their core beliefs absolutely are. This is not surprising, since most religions have merely canonized a few products of ancient ignorance and derangement and passed them down to us as though they were primordial truths. This leaves billions of us believing what no sane person could believe on his own. In fact, it is difficult to imagine a set of beliefs more suggestive

---

[47] Barker, *Godless,* 110.
[48] Andrews, *Deconverted*, 177.
[49] Barker, *Godless*, 40.
[50] Dennett, *Caught*, 34.
[51] Dawkins, *Delusion*, 28.

of mental illness than those that lie at the heart of many of our religious traditions.[52]

Much ink has been spilled by the New Atheists in their frustration over the continuing cultural acceptance for faith. While belief without evidence is sometimes considered a mark of madness, the atheist would argue that religious faith acts identically – yet manages to maintain a position of societal prestige.[53] Dawkins describes "the atonement, the central doctrine of Christianity, as vicious, sado-masochistic and repellent. We should also dismiss it as barking mad, but for its ubiquitous familiarity which has dulled our objectivity."[54]

Presumably unimpressed by the apostle Paul's assertion that spiritual things are discerned spiritually (1 Corinthians 2:14), atheists feel frustration when confronted with the apparent compartmentalization of irrational faith by otherwise reasonable men and women. How is it, they wonder, that in this single area of a man or woman's life, belief can float entirely free of reason or evidence?[55]

> *Most fundamentalist's... minds seem to have been partitioned to accommodate the profligate truth claims of their faith. Tell a devout Christian that his wife is cheating on him, or that frozen yogurt can make a man invisible, and he is likely to require as much evidence as anyone else, and to be persuaded only to the extent that you give it. Tell him that the book he keeps by his bed was written by an invisible deity who will punish him with fire for eternity if he fails to accept its every incredible claim about the universe, and he seem to require no evidence whatsoever.*[56]

God is Vicious and Wicked

Having sought to establish religion as both psychologically primitive as well as bearing all the marks of irrationality, the atheist's third and final attack on Christianity's intellectual viability may be broadly gathered under the category of the Biblical God's profound miscarriage of character. "The God of the Old Testament is arguably the most unpleasant character in all fiction: jealous and proud of it; a petty, unjust, unforgiving control-freak; a

---

[52] Harris, *End*, 113.
[53] Harris, *Letter*, 67.
[54] Dawkins, *Delusion*, 287.
[55] Harris, *End*, 17.
[56] Harris, *End*, 19.

vindictive, bloodthirsty ethnic cleanser; a misogynistic, homophobic, racist, infanticidal, genocidal, filicidal, pestilential, megalomaniacal, sadomasochistic, capriciously malevolent bully."[57]

Long before New Atheism was in vogue, Friedrich Nietzsche charged Christianity with a deep failure of morality. Seemingly oblivious to the requirement of Christian morality in order to charge its absence, Nietzsche stated, "Christianity has taken the side of everything weak, base, failed; it has made an ideal out of whatever *contradicts* the preservation instincts of a strong life; it has corrupted the reason of even the most spiritual natures by teaching people to see the slightest spiritual values as sinful, as deceptive, as *temptations*."[58] This line of thought is picked up and infused with modern sensibilities, charging the Noah's Ark story with genocide for instance, or Joshua's conquest of the Promised Land as ethnic cleansing.[59] Put simply, the New Atheists seem to be in agreement that following the Judeo-Christian God can rightly be viewed as the most potent source of human conflict.[60]

Over the years, a number of evangelical thinkers, at the forefront of their philosophical and theological fields, have stepped forward to counter the New Atheist's tone and accusations of stupidity, irrationality, or wickedness. In an uncharacteristically steaming rebuke, Alister McGrath, professor at the University of Oxford, argues that Richard Dawkins has become the very thing he opposes, a fundamentalist without any openness to the critique of his convictions nor a desire to actually understand what he rejects.[61] And Christian Philosopher Alvin Plantiga decries the New Atheists for their "proportion of insult, ridicule, mockery, spleen, and vitriol."[62] The penalty flag once thrown, however, has been largely ignored. A polemic of condescension and militancy is believed altogether appropriate to the atheist whose purpose is to unveil the believed,

---

[57] Dawkins, *Delusion*, 51.

[58] Friedrich Wilhelm Nietzsche, *The Anti-Christ, Ecce Homo, Twilight of the Idols* and *Other Writings*, ed. Aaron Ridley and Judith Norman (Cambridge: Cambridge University Press, 2005), 4-5.

[59] Dennett, *Caught*, 75.

[60] Harris, *End*, 35.

[61] Alister McGrath and Joanna Collicutt McGrath, *The Dawkins Delusion: Atheist Fundamentalism and the Denial of the Divine* (Downers Grove, IL.: InterVarsity, 2007), 68.

[62] Alvin Plantinga, "The Dawkins Confusion," accessed on April 11, 2015, http://www.christianitytoday.com/bc/2007/002/1.21.html.

insidious underpinning to Christianity. As the next section will set forward, such "revelation" is precisely their goal.

Section 5 of 5
Danger: Christianity, an Insidious Threat?

Having reviewed the development of New Atheism distinct from postmodernism, considered its common ground with Christianity, examined its striking departure from Christian morality, and heard its allegations of faith as absurdity, the Christian is at last able to perceive the end game coming into focus. Across the spectrum of 21st century atheism, a troubling thread begins to repeat: the accusation that Christianity is a clear and present danger to the further development of human society. This religious threat is believed to reveal itself in three primary ways: a quest for control, an impetus for wicked behavior, and a foundation for attack upon children.

Religion, a Means for Domination
If a tried and true polemic against Christian faith is to highlight her abuses and divergences from Biblical precept, then the hoped for eradication of Christian faith is comparable to abolishing sex abuse by first abolishing sex.[63] Nevertheless, this strategy is a common one. Edward Gibbon, in his 18th century classic *Decline and Fall of the Roman Empire* pointed out that various worship traditions in Rome were considered "by the people to be equally true, by the philosopher as equally false, and by the magistrate as equally useful."[64] This corrosive use of religion for domination is repeatedly noted by the New Atheists, drawing a tenuous connection between belief in an omniscient God and the desire to limit human liberty.   "It is no accident," Harris suggests, "that people of faith often want to curtail the private freedoms of others. This impulse has less to do with the history of religion and more to do with its logic, because the very idea of privacy is incompatible with the existence of God."[65]

---

[63] John F. Haught, *God and the New Atheism: A Critical Response to Dawkins, Harris, and Hitchens* (Louisville: Westminster, 2008), 37.

[64] Hitchens, *Great*, 155.

[65] Harris, 159.

New Atheism is virulent in its accusation against religion for societal ills as diverse as sexual repression,[66] the holocaust,[67] and a general impediment to building a global civilization.[68] Atheism is particularly pointed, however, in its combining all major religions together, followed by the attribution of world domination as the collective goal. "It can be stated as a truth that religion does not, and in the long run cannot, be content with its own marvelous claims and sublime assurances. It *must* seek to interfere with the lives of nonbelievers, or heretics, or adherents of other faiths. It may speak about the bliss of the next world, but it wants power in this one."[69] In the end, it would seem the atheist is convinced Napoleon Bonaparte spoke for all believers: "Religion is excellent stuff for keeping common people quiet."[70]

Religion, a Catalyst for Evil

One of the surprising discoveries when exploring New Atheism is her spokesperson's general disdain even for mild and moderate religious flavors. Rather than viewing liberal Christianity, for instance, as at least *less* of a bad thing (i.e. fundamentalist convictions), atheists are convinced that liberal religion provides the very climate of faith in which extremism naturally flourishes.[71] From there, it's only a matter of steps for Muriel Gray, writing in the Glasgow herald after the London bombings, to suggest, "Everyone is being blamed, from the obvious villainous duo of George W. Bush and Tony Blair, to the inaction of Muslim 'communities.' But it has never been clearer that there is only one place to lay the blame and it has never been thus. The cause of all this misery, mayhem, violence, terror, and ignorance is of course religion itself."[72]

A repeated error among atheists is to conflate belief in religious perversions as the equivalent of commitment to Biblical Christianity. Thus some will be assert that the suicide slaughter of innocents on 9/11 was perpetrated by the most "sincere believers" aboard the planes.[73] Likewise,

---

[66] Harris, 4.

[67] Harris, *Letter*, 41.

[68] Harris, *Letter*, 91.

[69] Hitchens, *Great*, 17.

[70] Ravi Zacharias, "The Religious Affiliation of Military and Political Leader Napoleon Bonaparte," accessed April 28, 2015, http://www.adherents.com/people/pn/Napoleon.html.

[71] Dawkins, *Delusion*, 342.

[72] Dawkins, *Delusion*, 343-344.

a Biblical view of eschatology will be twisted to an affirmation of apocalyptic savagery:

> With a necessary part of its collective mind, religion looks forward to the destruction of the world... It openly or covertly wishes that end to occur. Perhaps half aware that its unsupported arguments are not entirely persuasive, and perhaps uneasy about its own greedy accumulation of temporal power and wealth, religion has never ceased to proclaim the Apocalypse and the day of judgment... One of the very many connections between religious belief and the sinister, spoiled, selfish childhood of our species is the repressed desire to see everything smashed up and ruined and brought to naught... When the earthquake hits, or the tsunami inundates, or the twin towers ignite, you can see and hear the secret satisfaction of the faithful.[74]

Religion, a Path to Abuse

Following categorical attacks regarding desired domination and general wickedness, the New Atheist's final volley against faith is the most damaging – and certainly for the Christian, the most offensive. Time and again the point is made that concerted religious instruction, when systematically offered to a child or an adolescent, is equivalent to abuse.[75] Basic theological truths like the birth of Christ or substitutionary atonement are recast as the pathway to a life of spiritual servitude, tantamount to "Stockholm Syndrome for kindergarteners."[76]

> A tremendous amount of damage has been done in the name of religion. Children are psychologically scarred with fears of Hell. Homosexuals are ostracized for not fitting into the narrow "moral" confines molded by a church largely ignorant of human sexuality. Science classrooms are constantly fending off the advances of pseudo-scientists seeking to teach as fact an earth origin story involving six days, a dirt-man, a rib-woman, an enchanted tree and a talking snake.[77]

---

[73] Hitchens, *Great*, 32.
[74] Hitchens, *Great*, 56-57.
[75] Dennett, 172.
[76] Andrews, *Deconverted*, 5.
[77] Andrews, *Deconverted*, 160.

Richard Dawkins, the most well-known and widely read of the New Atheists, is also the most vociferous in his equation of religion and child abuse. Believing all religion to be nonsense, Dawkins sees no need to try and separate out one brand of nonsense from another; the concern is the same: once infected with religion, a child will grow up and infect the next generation with the same nonsense he or she received.[78] With that as the presupposition then, Dawkin's solution is distressing. He quotes with approval psychologist Nicholas Humphrey:

> In short, children have a right not to have their minds addled by nonsense, and we as a society have a duty to protect them from it. So we should no more allow parents to teach their children to believe, for example, in the literal truth of the Bible or that the planets rule their lives, than we should allow parents to knock their children's teeth out or lock them in a dungeon.[79]

Conclusions

The aim of New Atheism requires no careful reading between the lines; to their credit, 21st century atheistic leaders are bracingly clear regarding both intentions and strategies. Across the New Atheism spectrum, marginalizing Christianity unto obsolescence appears to be the goal. The "four horsemen of the non-apocalypse" may speak for themselves:

Christopher Hitchens: "Such stupidity, combined with such pride, should be enough on its own to exclude "belief" from the debate. The person who is certain, and who claims divine warrant for his certainty, belongs now to the infancy of our species. It may be a long farewell, but it has begun and, like all farewells, should not be protracted."[80]

Richard Dawkins: "The take-home message is that we should blame religion itself, not religious *extremism* – as though that were some

---

[78] Dawkins, *Delusion*, 219.
[79] Dawkins, *Delusion*, 367.
[80] Hitchens, *Great*, 11.

kind of terrible perversion of real, decent religion. Voltaire got it right long ago: "Those who can make you believe absurdities can make you commit atrocities." [81]

Daniel Dennett: "There are some famously arrogant Nobel laureates in the scientific community, but I have never encountered one who can hold a candle to the overweening confidence and smug certainty of the typical defender of the faith, whose disdain for evidence-seeking and careful argumentation is often breathtaking... They are incompetent to participate in the serious political conversations we ought to be engaging in today."[82]

Sam Harris: "Consider the case of alchemy: it fascinated human beings for over a thousand years, and yet anyone who seriously claims to be a practicing alchemist today will have disqualified himself for most positions of responsibility in our society. Faith-based religion must suffer the same slide into obsolescence."[83]

Since the dawn of church history, Christianity has faced diverse and sundry attacks – frequently upon its intellectual credentials and occasionally its very right to existence. When it comes to reading, understanding, and graciously responding to the newest attack – New Atheist ideology – the Bible-believing evangelical will be well served to recall the Apostle Paul's words to the Corinthian church: "Has not God made foolish the wisdom of the world?... Jews demand signs and Greeks seek wisdom, but we preach Christ crucified, a stumbling block to Jews and folly to Gentiles, but to those who are called, both Jews and Greeks, Christ the power of God and the wisdom of God" (1 Corinthians 1:20-24).

---

[81] Dawkins, *Delusion*, 345.
[82] Dennett, *Caught*, 224.
[83] Harris, *End*, 14.

CHAPTER TWO
The Grounding: Theological and Scriptural Foundations

Introduction

Prior to justification or substitutionary atonement or creation – before soteriology, hamartology, eschatology, or any other developed doctrine of the church – Scripture first offers the reader its simplest and most foundational truth: *there is a God.* To deny this, the Psalmist implies, is to deny the grounding of all reality: "The fool says in his heart, 'There is no God.'" (Psalm 14:1)   Given the Biblically assumed reality of the divine, what are the Scriptural and theological foundations that orthodox Christians can utilize when engaging with the New Atheism?

The skeptic may be encouraged to learn that throughout the Gospels, dubious disciples were often persuaded by Christ himself to evaluate evidence in the external world.   Nancy Pearcey, author of *Finding Truth,* points out that "robust responses are typical of Jesus. His ministry was a public work of question and answer and give and take. He set forth propositions that can be considered and discussed, and he invited people to observe public miracles that confirmed his claims in the here and now."[1] Facts, in other words, remain central to the Christian message.   Christianity

---

[1] Nancy Pearcey, *Finding Truth* (Colorado Springs, CO: David C. Cook, 2015), 16.

communicates not a mere belief system but it also conveys an accurate description of reality. And yet, the Apostle Paul warns God's people that they may be "outwitted by Satan" if they are "ignorant of his designs." (2 Cor 2:11)

Mark Twain famously described faith as "believing what you know ain't so." And yet, the Scriptural witness suggests quite the opposite: it is the unbeliever who often passively, and sometimes actively, shrouds the truth in a web of self-woven deceptions. Christian persuasion must always take into account the anatomy of an unbelieving mind in its denial of God. Someone once remarked, "Most present day Anglo-American philosophers have the same conception of reality as that held by a slightly drowsy, middle-aged businessman right after lunch."[2]

The Book of Romans, widely regarded as the systematic theology text of the Bible, contains in its first chapter what could be described as an apologetics training manual. In the study to follow, a ten verse section of this chapter will be offered as the Scripture's clearest and most cogent refutation of atheistic thought. Within Romans 1:16-25, one finds an unabashed declaration of the Gospel's power, followed by a step by step dissection of atheistic thought. This pericope will serve as home-base, the spine to which other Scriptural and theological foundations will then be referenced as connective tissue.

16 For I am not ashamed of the gospel, for it is the power of God for salvation to everyone who believes, to the Jew first and also to the Greek. 17 For in it the righteousness of God is revealed from faith for faith. As it is written, "The righteous shall live by faith. 18 For the wrath of God is revealed from heaven against all ungodliness and unrighteousness of men, who by their unrighteousness suppress the truth. 19 For what can be known about God is plain to them, because God has shown it to them. 20 For his invisible attributes, namely, his eternal power and divine nature, have been clearly perceived, ever since the creation of the world, in the things that have been made. So they are without excuse.

21 For although they knew God, they did not honor him as God or give thanks to him, but they became futile in their thinking, and their foolish hearts were darkened. 22 Claiming to be wise, they became fools, 23 and exchanged the glory of the immortal God for images resembling mortal man and birds and animals and creeping things. 24 Therefore God gave

---

[2] Peter L. Berger, *A Rumor of Angels* (New York: Anchor Books, 1970), 3.

them up in the lusts of their hearts to impurity, to the dishonoring of their bodies among themselves, 25 because they exchanged the truth about God for a lie and worshiped and served the creature rather than the Creator, who is blessed forever! Amen. (Romans 1:16-25)

Section 1 of 6
v18, Truth Suppressed (and fragmentation in its place)

According to Paul, the first step taken by the ungodly and unrighteous is to suppress the truth. "For the wrath of God is revealed from heaven against all ungodliness and unrighteousness of men, who by their unrighteousness suppress the truth." (Rom 1:18) If the branch of philosophy focused on the nature of knowledge is epistemology – how we know what we know – then humans have an epistemic duty to acknowledge truth and conform their lives to it. Romans 1 explains, however, that at the heart of the human condition there lies an epistemological sin – an outright refusal to acknowledge and rightly respond to what can be known about God.[3] Paul's autopsy of the human condition suggests that although God is constantly reaching out to his people through general revelation with evidence of his existence, humans are constantly suppressing those very same truths. "There comes a moment," C.S. Lewis once wrote, "when the children who have been playing at burglars hush suddenly: was that a real footstep in the hall? There comes a moment when people who have been dabbling in religion suddenly draw back. Supposing we really found Him?"[4]

All forms of unbelief, and certainly the New Atheism, are simply one form of truth-suppression followed by another. Materialists, for example, deny the reality of the mind while they use their *minds* to advocate for materialism. Determinists deny the reality of human choice while they *choose* to advocate for determinism. Relativists deny the existence of right and wrong while they *judge* those who disagree.[5]

---

[3] Pearcey, *Truth*, 34.
[4] C.S. Lewis, *Miracles* (New York: HarperCollins, 1974), 150.
[5] Pearcey, Truth, 19.

Reductionism

Reductionism, a particularly virulent form of truth-suppression, involves reducing a belief, idea, or concept from a higher or more complex level of reality to a lower, simpler, and less complex level (for example, reducing all of reality to mere naturalistic terms). The goal in reduction is to debunk the original concept. When it comes to the theist/atheist debate, compressing all of existence into a naturalistic understanding means that reductionism is "like trying to see the world through a single lens ... the result is always a vision of the world that is a narrower, poorer, darker and less humane than the biblical version."[6] In the case of the New Atheists, reality is commonly reduced to whatever can be empirically handled via reason and science, while simultaneously denying any observations that do not fit this reductionism. Those committed to naturalistic understanding may find themselves forced to categorize aspects of humanity – like human dignity and freedom – as mere illusion.[7]

In contrast to reductionism, a Christian worldview does *not* undermine human freedom or dignity. Christian epistemology intentionally grounds its starting point in a transcendent creator rather than self – "The fear of the *Lord* is the beginning of knowledge; fools despise wisdom and instruction." (Prov 1:7) Christian thought offers a significant distinction from skeptical thinkers, many of whom live a "two-story or bi-polar" existence. In their professional labors, the skeptic will adopt a reductionist philosophy, but when stepping out of the ivory towers of academia or leaving the corporate laboratory and returning home, the same individuals are then forced to a contrary paradigm where they of course treat people justly and humanely – *as if* they had inherent dignity.[8]

This two-story existence is a great challenge when dialoguing with New Atheism. Frank Turek offers a memorable word picture when he suggests that analyzing "atheist claims is like trying to gargle peanut butter. That's because we're exposing self-defeating statements... atheists often exempt themselves from their own claims and theories... if everyone is a molecular machine, then why do atheists act as if they can freely and reasonably arrive at atheistic conclusions?"[9]

---

[6] Pearcey, Truth, 137.

[7] Os Guinness, *Fool's Talk: Recovering The Art of Christian Persuasion* (Downers Grove, IL: InterVarsity Press, 2015), 75.

[8] Pearcey, *Truth*, 158.

[9] Frank Turek, *Stealing from God: Why Atheists Need God to Make Their Case* (Carol Stream, IL: NavPress, 2014), 14.

Thomas Nagel, a prominent atheist, is honest about the reality of truth-suppression in the form of reductionism when he observes fellow skeptics exempting themselves from the very reductionism they profess. The evolutionary concept of the mind undercuts "our confidence in the objective truth of our moral beliefs," as well as "the objective truth of our mathematical or scientific reasoning," the conviction that knowledge is "based ultimately on common sense and on what is plainly undeniable."[10] Atheist John Gray reluctantly observes something similar when he states, "Humanists never tire of preaching [the gospel of human freedom]. Darwin has shown us that we are animals... The idea of free will does not come from science." Humanism, he suggests, is just a secular version of Christian principles which renders the whole of western liberalism ultimately parasitic upon Christianity.[11]

Comfort with Contradiction

The way a worldview is tested in real time is by moving it out of the classroom into ordinary life. "Can it be lived out consistently in the real world, without doing violence to human nature? Does life function the way the worldview says it should? Does it fit reality?"[12] If Paul's original thesis is correct, and men by their unrighteousness have suppressed what is true, than a flawed worldview will in time begin to show cracks. For instance, when a real-world concept or conviction keeps inescapably bubbling into the mind of someone who denies it, that's a sure sign a general revelation truth is being actively suppressed.

It will surprise few orthodox Christians to discover that in their more authentic moments, multiple atheists have confessed to a disconnect between what is professed and what is felt. Dr. Paul Davis, an agnostic and respected cosmologist at the University of Arizona wrote in the *New York Times*, "Can the mighty edifice of physical order we perceive in the world about us ultimately be rooted in reasonless absurdity? If so, then nature is a fiendishly clever bit of trickery: meaninglessness and absurdity somehow masquerading as ingenious order and rationality."[13] Or consider Harvard psychologist Daniel Wegner who argues that even though all our actions

---

[10] Thomas Nagel, *Mind and Cosmos: Why the Materialist Neo-Darwinian Conception of Nature Is Almost Certainly False* (Oxford: Oxford University Press, 2012), 48-52.

[11] John Gray, *Straw Dogs* (New York: Farrar, Straus and Giroux, 2007), 49.

[12] Pearcey, *Truth*, 143.

[13] Paul Davies, "Taking Science on Faith," November 24, 2007, accessed January 14, 2016, http://www.nytimes.com/2007/11/24/opinion/24davies.html.

are actually the effects of unconscious physical causes, free will remains "a very persistent illusion; it keeps coming back... Even though you know it's a trick, you get fooled every time. The feelings just don't go away."[14]

Time and again the atheist is forced to suppress – and at times is honest about doing so – the very markers that materialism is not all there is. Edward Slingerland, in a section of his book ironically titled *We are Robots Designed Not to Believe that We are Robots* confesses, "We need to pull off the trick of living with a dual consciousness, cultivating the ability to view human beings simultaneously under two descriptions: as physical systems and as person."[15]   Marvin Minsky of MIT, best known for his description of the human brain as nothing but "a three pound computer of meat," admits that even though he believes the physical world to leave no room for freedom of the will, he cannot "ever give it up. We're virtually forced to maintain that belief, even though we know it's false."[16]

This is an important point: when someone talks about concepts they believe to be untrue, yet these same concepts are absolutely vital for a humane social order, that is a strong indicator the individual has bumped up against the edge of a reality that does not neatly fit inside their worldview.   They have opted for Pauline suppression, rather than acceptance, of the truth.   Rodney Brooks, a professor emeritus at MIT offers, "When I look at my children, I can, when I force myself ... see that they are machines ... That is not how I treat them ... I maintain two sets of inconsistent beliefs."[17]   Considering his own children, Slingerland similarly reveals a dualistic thought:

> At an important and ineradicable level, the idea of my daughter as merely a complex robot carrying my genes into the next generation is both bizarre and repugnant to me... There may well be individuals who lack this sense, and who can quite easily and thoroughly conceive of themselves and other people in purely instrumental, mechanistic terms, but we label such people 'psychopaths,' and quite rightly try to identify them and put them away somewhere to protect the rest of us."

[14] Daniel Wegner, *The Illusion of Conscious Will* (Cambridge, MA: Massachusetts Institute of Technology, 2002), 156.

[15] Edward Slingerland, *What Science Offers the Humanities: Integrating Body and Culture* (New York: Cambridge University Press, 2008), 289.

[16] Marvin Minsky, *The Society of Mind* (New York: Simon & Schuster, 1986), 307.

[17] Rodney Brooks, *Flesh and Machines: How Robots Will Change Us* (New York: Pantheon, 2002), 174.

Does this fit reality? Should someone who *accurately* assesses their fellow humans be labeled a psychopath? Albert Einstein recognizes the dichotomy: "Human beings in their thinking, feeling, and acting, are not free but are as causally bound as the stars in their motions." And yet, he admits, "I am compelled to act as if free will existed because if I want to live in a civilized society I must act responsibly."[18]

What all this means is that many, perhaps most, atheists are living fragmented lives. When one has to actively choose, month after month and year after year, to disbelieve what gut instinct shouts out to be true, the result is individuals and culture that lack integration. Philosopher Louis Dupre observes, "We experience our culture as fragmented; we live on bits of meaning and lack the overall vision that holds them together in a whole."[19]

Section 2 of 6
v19-20, Natural Revelation Suppressed (and materialism in its place)

Within the apologetics training manual that is Romans 1, Paul now moves to his second indictment of the atheistic conception of reality – an intentional ignorance of Natural Revelation. "For what can be known about God is plain to them, because God has shown it to them. For his invisible attributes, namely, his eternal power and divine nature, have been clearly perceived, ever since the creation of the world, in the things that have been made. So they are without excuse." (Rom 1:19-20)

If God's nature and character are revealed to mankind via two distinct streams, then General Revelation is the first (Special Revelation, or supernatural revelation like Scripture, being the second). "The heavens declare the glory of God," the Psalmist shouts, "and the sky above proclaims his handiwork. Day to day pours out speech, and night to night reveals knowledge." (Ps 19:1-2) General Revelation alone, clear for all to see and apart even from the Special Revelation of God's redemptive

---

[18] Walter Isaacson, *Einstein: His Life and Universe* (New York: Simon & Schuster, 2007), 391-392.

[19] "Seeking Christian Interiority: An Interview with Louis Dupre," *Christian Century*, July 16-23, 1997, Accessed February 16, 2016, https://www.questia.com/magazine /1G1-19651878/seeking-christian-interiority-an-interview-with-louis.

purpose, is enough to leave humanity inexcusable. The Westminster Divines offered a clear summary of these truths as the opening words to their Reformation era confession: "The light of nature, and the works of creation and providence do so far manifest the goodness, wisdom, and power of God, as to leave men inexcusable."[20]

The theological category of General Revelation is a key one for dialogue with atheists; one might suggest that a mind capable of forming an argument *against* God's existence constitutes evidence *for* his existence. "He who planted the ear, does he not hear? He who formed the eye, does he not see?" (Ps 94:9). Biologist Ariel Roth frames the discussion neatly: "God never performed a miracle to convince an atheist, because His ordinary works can provide sufficient evidence."[21]

Materialism Introduced

For each step of truth suppression that Paul marks out in Romans 1, something is inevitably offered by the unbeliever to fill its place. In the place of General Revelation, the prevailing view among New Atheists and much of the academic world is naturalistic materialism. Materialism demands that what is ultimately real – in fact, the only thing that is real – is molecules in motion. Materialism is philosophically committed to the dogma that physics is sufficient to explain chemistry, chemistry is sufficient to explain biology, and biology is sufficient to explain the human mind.[22] Most atheists accept a worldview which says only material things exist. This inevitably leads, as will be reviewed later on, to some form of scientism – the belief that science will ultimately answer any and all questions about the natural world as well as the human condition.[23]

As with most false gods, Materialism contains a kernel of truth because God did in fact create a material universe. He even pronounced it "very good." (Gen 1:31) But Materialism recognizes only a piece of reality. Returning to the earlier two-story framework,[24] material reductionists necessarily live in only one story – the empirically tested universe. They treat matter and energy as the only things that are real, knowable, and

---

[20] The Westminster Confession of Faith, accessed January 15, 2016, http://www.opc.org/wcf.html#Chapter_01.

[21] Ariel Roth, *Origins* (Hagerstown, MD: Herald, 1998), 94.

[22] Pearcey, *Truth*, 70.

[23] Andy Bannister, *The Atheist Who Didn't Exist, Or: the Dreadful Consequences of Bad Arguments* (Oxford, England: Monarch Books, 2015), 41.

[24] See page 36.

objectively true. Likewise, the materialist forces into the upper story everything that does not fit the naturalist box – soul, morality, love, eternal purpose.[25] This two-story existence eventually forces the "consistent" unbeliever to uncomfortable conclusions. "Our starting assumption as scientists ought to be that on some level consciousness has to be an illusion," says Cambridge psychologist Nicholas Humphrey. "The reason is obvious: If nothing in the physical world can have the features that consciousness seems to have, then consciousness cannot exist as a thing in the physical world."[26]

The Self Defeating Materialist

C.S. Lewis, originally writing during the Second World War, accurately identified the self-defeating nature of materialistic rationalism. "If minds are wholly dependent on brains, and brains on biochemistry, and biochemistry (in the long run) on the meaningless flux of the atoms, I cannot understand how the thought of those minds should have any more significance than the sound of the wind in the trees."[27] The enigma is obvious. Individuals who cannot trust their own thinking cannot then trust the arguments leading to atheism – which leaves them little reason to be atheists. Reductionists, ultimately, cannot reason within the confines of their own worldview box, so they smuggle in ladders from a Christian worldview in order to climb back out.[28]

John Lennox, a professor of mathematics at the University of Oxford, writes that according to atheism, "the mind that does science … is the end product of a mindless unguided process. Now, if you knew your computer was the product of a mindless unguided process, you wouldn't trust it. So, to me atheism undermines the rationality I need to do science."[29] So how do materialist atheists avoid Lennox's self-refuting conclusion? In one form or another, they all make a tacit exception for their beliefs, trusting their own thinking. Atheists necessarily exempt themselves from their own reductive categories of analysis. Atheist Thomas Nagel admits the contradiction: "Evolutionary naturalism provides an account of our

[25] Pearcey, *Truth*, 104.

[26] Cited in John Brockman, ed., *Intelligent Thought: Science versus the Intelligent Design Movement* (New York, Vintage, 2006), 58.

[27] C.S. Lewis, *The Weight of Glory* (New York: HarperCollins, 1976), 139.

[28] Pearcey, *Truth*, 220.

[29] Cited in Victoria Gill, " Big Bang: Is There Room for God?," *BBC News,* October 19, 2012.

capacities that undermines their reliability, and in doing so undermines itself."[30]

Consider the following illustration to reveal the bankruptcy of materialist thinking. Metal detectors used on the beach, though quite useful for locating items buried in the sand, can't find everything. They're useless at locating wood, plastic, rubber or any other nonmetallic objects. Yet imagine the man who confidently proclaims there is *nothing* on the beach except metal – because only metal has been found. Atheists often function like the confused man in the illustration. Because their scientific (i.e. materialist) tools are successful at discovering material causes in the natural world, they mistakenly assume nothing but material things exist. Edward Feser, who developed this illustration, explains the end result. You can't take a materialist methodology for discovering truth and say it's the only method. The man who does, Feser writes, "is like the drunk who thinks his car keys *must* be under the lamppost because that is the only place there is light to look for them – and who refuses to listen to those who have already found them elsewhere."[31]

For a materialist, the laws of physics determine everything that humans think and do. And yet if this is the case, then individuals have no justification to believe anything they think, including the conviction that atheism is true. "Where is the one who is wise? Where is the scribe? Where is the debater of this age? Has not God made foolish the wisdom of the world? For since, in the wisdom of God, the world did not know God through wisdom, it pleased God through the folly of what we preach to save those who believe." (1 Cor 1:20-21)

The Limits of Materialism

Once the limits of materialism are recognized, the atheistic convictions for rationalism, Scientism, and Darwinian evolution begin to unravel. The theory of natural selection, for instance, is often viewed as holding an *a priori* commitment to materialism that intentionally rules out intelligent design or the supernatural from consideration. It is not based on a philosophically neutral assessment of the evidence. In their book *I Don't Have Enough Faith to Be An Atheist*, the authors helpfully invite the reader

---

[30] Nagel, *Cosmos,* 27.
[31] Edward Feser, "Not Understanding Nothing: A Review of *A Universe from Nothing*," June 20, 2012, accessed January 15, 2016, https://www.firstthings.com/article/2012/06/not-understanding-nothing.

back in time.

If we could watch a video recording of the history of the universe in reverse, we would see all matter in the universe collapse back to a point, not the size of a basketball, not the size of a golf ball, not even the size of a pinhead, but mathematically and logically to a point that is actually nothing... The Big Bang was the beginning point for the entire physical universe. Time, space, and matter came into existence at that point. There was no natural world or natural law prior to the Big Bang. Since a cause cannot come after its effect, natural forces cannot account for the Big Bang. Therefore, there must be something outside of nature to do the job. That's exactly what the word supernatural means.[32]

This is where the Apostle Paul chose to begin his dialogue with the Athenian Areopagus. Recognizing there was something they did not know, Paul stepped to the microphone, as it were, and offered a gracious invitation. "I found also an altar with this inscription, 'To the unknown god.' What therefore you worship as unknown, this I proclaim to you. The God who made the world and everything in it..." (Acts 17:23-24)

Section 3 of 6
V21, Divine Authority Suppressed (and scientism in its place)

In his letter to the Roman church, Paul continues his autopsy of atheistic thought by addressing the desire to supplant God's sovereign reign with alternative – and more manageable – authorities. "For although they knew God, they did not honor him as God or give thanks to him, but they became futile in their thinking, and their foolish hearts were darkened." (Rom 1:21) In the 21st century New Atheist context, the preferred replacement authority to divine rule is typically Scientism.

Most atheists believe in naturalism, a worldview which suggests it is only material things which exist. Many atheists also believe in some form of scientism, the belief that science can (ultimately, if not yet) answer any and all questions – both about the natural world and about the human condition.[33] This belief system accepts not one but two false premises: no

---

[32] Norman L. Geisler and Frank Turek, *I Don't Have Enough Faith to Be an Atheist* (Wheaton, Illinois: Crossway, 2004), 79 and 85.

theistic evidence *exists* and a great deal of atheistic evidence *does*.

Is Science the Highest Authority?

History may aptly be described as the repeated story of man committing cosmic treason. "All the inhabitants of the earth are accounted as nothing, and [God] does according to his will among the host of heaven and among the inhabitants of the earth." (Daniel 4:35) Science is a tremendous tool for advancement and the benefit of mankind. However, when science is treated as the sole or highest source of truth, then it becomes another false God and fulfillment of Paul's Romans 1:21 declaration.

The unreasonable elevation of science is precisely what has been witnessed among numerous atheists in the past 100 years. Philosopher Wilfrid Sellars expressed, "Science is the measure of all things."[34] Bertrand Russell predicts, "What science cannot discover, mankind cannot know."[35] Richard Dawkins claims, "Scientists [are] the specialists in discovering what is true about the world and the universe."[36] Harry Kroto, a Nobel Prize-winning chemist states, "Science is the only philosophical construct we have to determine truth with any degree of reliability."[37] And leading chemist Peter Atkins believes, "Humanity should be proud that he has actually stumbled into this way of understanding the world and that it really can attack every problem that concerns humanity with the prospect of an outcome. Science also gives you the promise of understanding while you're alive, whilst religion offers the prospect of understanding when you are dead."[38]

What motive might lie beneath the nearly God-like status ascribed by so many to the scientific endeavor? Contemporary philosopher Thomas Nagel is candid when he offers, "I want atheism to be true and am made

---

[33] Bannister, *Exist*, 41.

[34] Wilfred Sellars, *Science, Perception, and Reality* (Atascadero, CA: Ridgeview, 1991), 173

[35] Bertrand Russell, *Science and Religion* (Oxford: Oxford University Press, 1935), 235.

[36] Richard Dawkins, *A Devil's Chaplain: Selected Writings* (London: Phoenix Press, 2004), 242.

[37] Cited by Andre Brown, "Science is the only road to truth? Don't be absurd" July 4, 2011, accessed on January 22, 2016, http://www.theguardian.com/commentisfree/andrewbrown/2011/jul/04/harry-kroto-science-truth

[38] Peter Atkins, *Burning Questions* TV documentary, Episode 2: "God and Science", accessed February 16, 2016, http://www.burningquestions.ca

uneasy by the fact that some of the most intelligent and well-informed people I know are religious believers. It isn't just that I don't believe in God and, naturally, hope that I'm right in my belief. It's that I hope there is no God! I don't want there to be a God; I don't want the universe to be like that."[39] It's been said that "to a man with a hammer, everything is a nail." Likewise, in an age of science and technology, for many it would seem that everything is a scientific and technical matter that must be solved by scientific and technical means.[40] Yet Nagel's quote above gives insight into the driving forces behind this tendency. It is no surprise that irritation follows where authority is lost. "We prefer a user-friendly God – one that purrs when we pet him."[41] Apart from a regenerate heart, mankind will always opt for a God that can be controlled, rather than a God who is in control.

Scientism is ultimately another form of reductionism. It is the chosen epistemology that loads the premises from the outset to avoid the possibility of a God who stands above humanity. Emma Goldman suggests that the concept of God "has dominated humanity and will continue to do so until man will raise his head to the sunlit day, unafraid and with an awakened will to himself... How far man will be able to find his relation to his fellows will depend entirely upon how much he can outgrow his dependence upon God."[42]

Peter Hitchens, Christian brother to the late New Atheist Christopher Hitchens, offers a potent diagnosis of the authority issue:

> My guess is that this cosmic authority problem is not a rare condition and that it is responsible for much of the scientism and reductionism of our time. One of the tendencies it supports is the ludicrous overuse of evolutionary biology to explain everything about life, including everything about the human mind ... Without God, many more actions are possible than are permitted in a Godly order. Atheism is a license for ruthlessness, and it appeals to the ruthless.[43]

---

[39] Thomas Nagel, *The Last Word* (New York: Oxford University Press, 1997), 130.

[40] Guinness, *Fool's*, 31.

[41] Norman L. Geisler, and Daniel J. McCoy, *The Atheist's Fatal Flaw: Exposing Conflicting Beliefs* (Grand Rapids: Baker Books, 2014), 155.

[42] Emma Goldman, "The Philosophy of Atheism," in *The Portable Atheist: Essential Readings for the Nonbelievers*, edited by Christopher Hitchens (Philadelphia: Da Capo Press, 2007), 130.

[43] Peter Hitchens, *The Rage Against God: How Atheism Led Me to Faith* (Grand

C.S. Lewis poetically identifies the God we want versus the God who is: "We want, in fact, not so much a Father in Heaven as a grandfather in heaven – a senile benevolence who, as they say, 'liked to see young people enjoying themselves,' and whose plan for the universe was simply that it might be truly said at the end of the day, 'a good time was had by all.'"[44]

The Absence of Atheistic Evidence

Despite the dogmatic claims of the New Atheists, there is a shockingly small amount of evidence to support a naturalistic and materialistic view of the universe. Francis Crick, best known for cracking the DNA code in 1953, was a devout atheist who later undertook to disprove the existence of the soul or self. Crick struggled, however, with the dissonance of a world he believed to be entirely naturalistic yet at the same time showed apparent signs of design. "Biologists must constantly keep in mind that what they see was not designed, but rather evolved."[45] Crick felt the need to encourage vigilance against intelligent design because the more science has developed, the more clues it suggests for a creator who stands *outside* the natural order. Perhaps the most significant piece of evidence is the irrefutable discovery that the universe had a beginning.

Agnostic cosmologist Alexander Vilenkin admits, "It can't possibly be eternal in the past. There must be some kind of boundary... It is said that an argument is what convinces reasonable men and a proof is what it takes to convince even an unreasonable man. With the proof now in place, cosmologists can no longer hide behind the possibility of a past-eternal universe. There is no escape, they have to face the problem of a cosmic beginning."[46] Against the backdrop of a non-eternal universe, an oft-overlooked truth of atheism begins to emerge: it is a worldview with numerous beliefs held by faith in things unseen. Atheists don't merely lack belief in God, they actively believe in various unproven and non-evidenced theories to explain reality without God. To claim that atheism is not a worldview is like suggesting anarchy is not a political position.[47]

To illustrate the point, the multiverse theory is a relatively recent hypothesis that billions of universes exist, thus rendering it more "likely"

Rapids, MI: Zondervan, 2010), 140 & 150.

[44] C.S. Lewis, *The Problem of Pain* (New York: Macmillan, 1944), 31.

[45] Francis Crick, *What Mad Pursuit: A Personal View of Scientific Discovery* (New York: Basic Books, 1988), 138.

[46] Alexander Vilenkin, *Many Worlds in One* (New York: Hill and Wang, 2006), 176.

[47] Turek, *Stealing*, xxiii.

for one in which life arises by chance (i.e the universe in which these words were typed). And yet even agnostic astronomer Paul Davies is quick to confess that the multiverse theory – a hypothesis for which absolutely no evidence exists – is ultimately a "dodge." It's a theory developed to explain the incomprehensibly fine-tuned universe around us absent a creator.[48] And even here, in a leap of quite literally *universal* proportions, Vilenkin (himself a proponent of the multiverse) admits that if other universes exist, the entire multiverse would still require an absolute beginning.[49] Standing opposite the skeptic's theories, Scripture shows us the way back home: "And he is before all things, and in him all things hold together." (Colossians 1:17)

The Presence of Theistic Evidence

Against both the backdrop of scientism and the evidence lacking for an atheistic conception of reality, one will find the vacuum quickly fills with evidence *for* a theistic worldview. "You are the Lord, you alone. You have made heaven, the heaven of heavens, with all their host, the earth and all that is on it, the seas and all that are in them; and you preserve all of them; and the host of heaven worships you." (Neh 9:6)

The conversation surrounding universal origin has given rise to a puzzle known as the fine-tuning problem. The observable world, and most certainly any living system, is an irreducibly complex system. A car engine serves as a helpful example of what is meant here. In the context of a vehicle, any change made to the size of the pistons would require simultaneous changes in the cam shaft, block, cooling system, engine compartment, and other systems – or the new engine would not function.[50] Irreducible complexity, similarly witnessed in all living systems but on an exponentially grander scale, serves as impressive evidence for theistic design. Force of Gravity, the strong nuclear force, the weak nuclear force, the electromagnetic force, ratio of the mass and proton and electron – all these fall within what cosmologists call the goldilocks dilemma. "These mysterious numbers...are like the knobs on God's control console, and they seem almost miraculously tuned to allow life."[51] Stephen Hawking

---

[48] Cited in Turek, *Stealing*, 50.

[49] Lisa Grossman, "Why Physicists Can't Avoid a Creation Event," January 11, 2012, accessed on January 22, 2016, https://www.newscientist.com/article/mg21328474-400-why-physicists-cant-avoid-a-creation-event/.

[50] Geisler, *Enough*, 145.

[51] Dennis Overbye, "Zillions of Universes? Or Did Ours Get Lucky?," October 28,

estimates that if the expansion rate of the universe was different by one part in a hundred thousand million million, one second after the big bang, the universe would have either collapsed back on itself or never developed galaxies.[52]

The significant truth here is that evidence like the goldilocks dilemma is no mere "God of the gaps" argument, using divinity to fill in the holes of ignorance. It's not simply that atheism fails to explain irreducible complexity, universal-fine tuning, or multiverse origins. The key point is that each of these items serve as positive, timeless, and unchanging evidence for an intelligent creator-being.   John Lennox observes, "Postulating an unobserved Designer is no more unscientific than postulating unobserved macro-evolutionary steps." And Stephen Meyers adds:

> Physicists postulate forces, fields, and quarks; biochemists infer submicroscopic structures; psychologists discuss their patients' mental states. Evolutionary biologists themselves infer unobserved past mutations and invoke the existence of extinct organisms and transitional forms for which no fossils remain. Such things, like the actions of an intelligent designer, are inferred from observable evidence in the present, because of the explanatory power they may offer.[53]

"All these things my hand has made, and so all these things came to be, declares the Lord." (Isaiah 66:2)   While the prophet Isaiah may not offer compelling evidence to the convinced atheist, this Lord who made "all these things" has offered copious evidence in natural revelation alone. Antony Flew was one of the most widely known atheist philosophers of the last century. He never became a Christian, nor chose to believe in an afterlife; however, in 2004 (after years of writing to support atheism) Flew announced he had become a theist. In his case, the evidence was provided by DNA – ironically, the very thing discovered by atheist Francis Crick. "What I think the DNA material has done," Flew said at a symposium at New York University, "is that it has shown, by the almost unbelievable complexity of the arrangements which are needed to produce life, that intelligence must have been involved in getting these extraordinarily

---

2003, accessed on January 22, 2016.   *http://www.nytimes.com/2003/10/28/ science/space/28COSM.html?pagewanted=all.*

[52]   William Lane Craig, *Reasonable Faith* (Wheaton, IL: Crossway, 2008), 157-172.

[53]   Stephen C. Meyer, *Darwin's Doubt* (New York: HarperCollins, 2013), 389.

diverse elements to work together."[54]

The reality, perfectly exemplified by the Flew/Crick juxtaposition, is that both theistic and atheistic scientists are looking at the same evidence. This means that often the real debate is about how to interpret the evidence, and interpretation involves philosophical commitments about what causes will be considered possible. Materialists rule out an intelligent designer cause in advance, and therefore render themselves unable to properly interpret natural revelation if an intelligent being is in fact responsible. "No philosophy is completely disinterested," Aldous Huxley once confessed, "The pure love of truth is always mingled to some extent with the need, consciously or unconsciously by even the noblest and most intelligent philosophers, to justify a given form of personal or social behavior."[55] In the end, science may tell us what is. Only the God of the Bible can tell us what ought to be.

Section 4 of 6
V22, Objective Morality Suppressed (and situational ethics in its place)

What is versus *what ought to be* — this distinction lies at an epi-center of New Atheism's weakness: the origin and validity of moral systems. The apostle Paul predicted this confusion in Romans when he penned the simple statement, "Claiming to be wise, they became fools..." (Romans 1:22) The Biblical witness repeatedly sets forth mankind's attempt to displace the wisdom of God with the wisdom of man. Seven hundred years before Christ, Isaiah wrote, "Woe to those who call evil good and good evil, who put darkness for light and light for darkness, who put bitter for sweet and sweet for bitter!" (Isaiah 5:20) Isaiah's curse was nothing more than the fruit of Satan's first recorded question, "Did God really say...?" (Genesis 3:1)

The Shifting Sands of a Godless Morality
Not altogether dissimilar to Satan's methodology when inciting the

---

54 Antony Flew, *There Is a God: How the World's Most Notorious Atheist Changed His Mind* (New York: HarperOne, 2007), 75.

55 Aldous Huxley, "Beliefs," in *Ends and Means: An Inquiry into the Nature of Ideals* (Piscataway, NJ: Transaction Publishers, 2012), 312.

first recorded sin, the assumption among atheism is that true morality, like mathematics, may be discovered by rationality alone. God's voice is questioned at the start, ignored in the end, and the wisdom of men – *a la* Paul in Romans 1:22 – becomes a sorry imposter. Bertrand Russell, a tremendously influential atheist in the 20th century implies any additional morality not rationally determined by mankind must be left behind:

> *It is evident that a man with a scientific outlook on life cannot let himself be intimidated by texts of Scripture or by the teaching of the church. He will not be content to say "such-and-such an act is sinful, and that ends the matter." He will inquire whether it does any harm or whether, on the contrary, the belief that it is sinful does harm. And he will find that, especially in what concerns sex, our current morality contains a very great deal of which the origin is purely superstitious.*[56]

The *Christian* conception of reality is far removed from Russell's, for it is one in which morality is not determined by majority vote. Morality, it may be suggested, is not determined at all. Individuals do not determine the right thing or the wrong thing – they discover it. John Gray, former professor of European Thought at the London School of Economics and no fan of religion, has something very interesting to say in his book *Heresies:* "Liberal humanism is a secular rendition of a Christian myth, but the truth in the myth has been lost on the way. The biblical story of the Fall teaches that evil cannot be rooted out from human life. Humans are radically flawed – a perception rooted in the doctrine of Original Sin. It is not error or ignorance that stands in the way of a better world. The human animal may yearn for peace and freedom, but it is no less fond of war and tyranny."[57]

Atheists cannot justify morality and be consistent with their professed worldview. This is not to suggest many do not in fact act morally, consistent in numerous ways with a Judeo-Christian ethic. However, in judging some actions as moral and others as immoral, the atheist is unable to provide an objective basis for those judgments. Atheism, as has already been stated, is not an absence of belief; rather, it is a worldview with the positive belief that man is ultimately nothing more than molecules. For this reason, none other than Richard Dawkins admits he is anti-Darwinian when it comes to morality. "I've always said that I am a passionate anti-

---

[56] Bertrand Russell, *Why I Am Not a Christian* (New York: Touchstone, 1957), 65-66.

[57] John Gray, *Heresies: Against Progress and Other Illusions* (London: Granta, 2004), 8.

Darwinian when it comes to the way we should organize our lives and our morality ... We want to avoid basing our society on Darwinian principles."[58] And Friedrich Nietzsche, one of the most famous atheists in the past 200 years, long ago saw the implications of naturalistic theory on moralistic philosophy: "When one gives up the Christian faith, one pulls the right to Christian morality out from under one's feet. This morality is by no means self-evident... Christianity is a system, a whole view of things thought out together. By breaking one main concept out of it, the faith in God, one breaks the whole: nothing necessary remains in one's hands."[59]

So in the context of morality and with reference to Romans 1:22, what is the foolishness of man that is offered in the place of God's wisdom? Among the New Atheists, the most developed moralistic theory is offered by Sam Harris. In his book *The Moral Landscape*, Harris pushes back on the belief that objective moral values do not exist. Rather, he asserts that objective truths in the moral sphere can be known, and no need exists to invoke God. If we simply use reason, then "human flourishing" will be seen as the obvious standard by which something is determined to be good or bad. Objective morality is tightly woven to the well-being of conscious creatures.

> *Questions about values – about meaning, morality, and life's larger purpose – are really questions about the well-being of conscious creatures. Values, therefore, translate into facts that can be scientifically understood...If there are objective truths to be known about human well-being – if kindness, for instance, is generally more conducive to happiness than cruelty is – then science should one day be able to make very precise claims about which of our behaviors and uses of attention are morally good, which are neutral, and which are worth abandoning.[60]*

The reasoning Harris offers sounds quite convincing – right up until the point of serious reflection. Both individuals and societies are sociologically and historically inconsistent in their view of what constitutes "well-being" for sentient humans. Astounding atrocities have been committed by the

---

[58] Ian Boyne, Why God Might Exist, March 8, 2015, Accessed on January 26, 2016, http://jamaica-gleaner.com/article/focus/20150308/ian-boyne-why-god-might-exist

[59] Friedrich Nietzsche, *Twilight of the Idols and the Anti-Christ* (London: Penguin, 2003), 80-81.

[60] Sam Harris, *The Moral Landscape: How Science Can Determine Human Values* (New York: Free Press, 2011), 1-2, 8.

one in favor of another's "well-being." Andy Bannister replies, "The Moral Zeitgeist, it turns out, is not so much a sawtooth as a crazily scribbled line, drawn in crayon by a toddler on a sugar rush. It seems that we're no better off leaving society to determine what "good" and "evil" look like than we are allowing individuals to do so."[61]

The Existence of Evil

Predicting the implications of morality unhinged from an objective creator, Nietzsche prophesied that killing belief in God in the 1800's would result in the mass killing of humans in the 1900's. This, of course, is precisely what occurred. Dinesh D'Souza offers the sobering perspective that in just a few decades, Stalin, Hitler, and Mao together murdered tens of millions of people. By contrast, over a 500 year period, the Crusades, the Inquisition, and witch burnings together were responsible for perhaps 200,000 deaths – less than 1 percent of the totals in the atheistic nation-states.[62]

Few would hesitate to label the aforementioned atrocities as "evil," but one must think through the grounding and implications of such a term. Evil, rightly defined, cannot exist on its own. It exists as deficiency in a good thing. Turek offers the analogy of evil like rust in a car. When one removes all the rust from a vehicle, that which is left is simply a better car. However, if one could take the car out of the rust, what's left is nothing. In a similar way, evil as a concept only has definition when seen against the backdrop of good things. Even English vocabulary reflects this truth: _im_moral, _un_just, _un_fair, _dis_honest.

The reality of Paul's Romans 1:22 warning about wisdom traded for foolishness begins to come clear. When the objective beauty of a good God is removed from the equation, evil as a category becomes nebulous and floating.

At the outset of World War II, the poet W.H. Auden was an atheistic, homosexual, left-wing socialist. Long before he eventually professed Christianity however, Auden was struck by the inconsistency in a morality detached from objective truth. "Unless one is prepared to take a relativist view that all morals are a matter of personal taste, one could hardly avoid asking the question: 'If, as I am convinced, the Nazis are wrong and we are

---

[61] Bannister, _Exist_, 151.
[62] Dinesh D'Souza, _What's So Great about Christianity_ (Washington, DC: Regnery, 2007), 214-215.

right, what is it that validates our values and invalidates theirs?"[63]

Auden, in the quote above, was touching on Scriptural truth. To be effectively absolute, a moral code must be beyond human power to alter. This maxim, however, leads to a larger question: *who decides what is good?* Only the answer to this question can consequently determine who decides what is evil. Peter Hitchens points out that Soviet communism, for instance, was "organically linked to atheism, materialist rationalism, and most of the other causes that New Atheists support. It used the same language, treasured the same hopes, and appealed to the same constituency as atheism... [Atheists] fear that, by admitting their delight at the non-existence of good and evil, they are revealing something of their motives for their belief. Could it be that the last thing on earth they wish to acknowledge is that they *have* motives for their belief?"[64]

Morality Rooted in God or Nothing At All

For a moral code to be effective, Scripture reminds us that it must be vested in a non-human source. "The sum of your word is truth, and every one of your righteous rules endures forever." (Psalm 119:160) A moral code must be outside the power of humanity to change it, to satisfy passing whim and preference.

The Christian worldview interprets each breaking of the moral law as a slap in the face of God. However, once morality is redefined absent God's involvement, such a breaking of the law merely slaps the air. Sam Harris suggests, "It is time we realized that crimes without victims are like debts without creditors."[65] And Michael Onfray, in his Atheist Manifesto, could not agree more: "God was not content with that one prohibition on the forbidden fruit. Ever since, he has revealed himself to us only through taboos. The monotheistic religions live exclusively by prescriptions and constraints: things to do and things not to do, to say and not to say, think and not to think, perform and not to perform."[66]

A common theme among the New Atheists is their tendency to "double-dip" on the morality accusation, thereby invalidating the argument. On the one hand they indict God for the not fixing the problem

---

[63] Arthur Kirsch, *Auden and Christianity* (Sheridan Books, 2005), 22.

[64] Hitchens, *Rage*, 137 & 149.

[65] Sam Harris, *The End of Faith: Religion, Terror, and the Future of Reason* (New York: W.W. Norton & Company Inc, 2004), 171.

[66] Michael Onfray, *Atheist Manifesto: The Case Against Christianity, Judaism, and Islam* (New York: Arcade Publishing, 2008), 69-70.

of moral evil, frustrated at a world where evil exists. On the other hand, they are quick to indict God for his attempts to fix it, frustrated that a personal God would in any way offer directions or prohibitions. Somehow, as Onfray's quote above illustrates, God is accused of immorality both for being too permissive and then for being too inhibiting.

The reality is that if there is no God, and no afterlife, then morality has no fixed grounding. Crimes, even great crimes, are ultimately labeled such with nothing more than the weight of strong opinion. In addition, if there is no God and no afterlife, justice can never be done. For instance, thousands of pedophiles who have committed murder over the years without being caught will never receive justice. "Too bad," said Richard Dawkins in a debate with Oxford mathematician John Lennox. "Just because we wish there was ultimate justice, doesn't mean there is."[67] This statement is true as far as it goes, but Dawkins once again misses the inverse – if justice does not exist, neither can *in*justice.

Every moral law known to man has a law giver. This is intuitive to virtually all people – no legislation can be passed without a legislature. Similarly, if moral obligations exist, there must be someone to be obligated to.[68] A man does not call a line crooked unless he has some idea of a straight line. If something is labeled unjust, whose basis of justice will be used? C.S. Lewis was led, by this very realization, out of atheism and into Christianity. Paul implied in Romans 1:22 that wisdom will be feigned but foolishness will reign. C.S. Lewis expands upon the same point, revealing the absurdity of expecting virtue from people who are taught that no virtue exists: "In a sort of ghastly simplicity we remove the organ and demand the function. We make men without chests and expect of them virtue and enterprise. We laugh at honor and are shocked to find traitors in our midst. We castrate and bid the geldings be fruitful."[69]

Section 5 of 6
V23, God's Glory Suppressed (and nihilism in its place)

Paul's Romans 1 dissection of unbelief reveals an uncomfortable consequence of atheistic philosophy. When the glory of God's sovereign

---

[67] Turek, *Stealing*, 90.
[68] Geisler, *Flaw*, 171.
[69] C.S. Lewis, *The Abolition of Man* (New York: MacMillan, 1947), 35.

rule is suppressed, as it must be when His existence is denied, nihilism is the only rational system that can be offered in its place. "[They] exchanged the glory of the immortal God for images resembling mortal man and birds and animals and creeping things." (Romans 1:23)

Nihilism, which entails the rejection of all religion and religiously-rooted moral principles, is a philosophical doctrine that denies ultimately meaningful aspects of life. This form of extreme pessimism and radical skepticism is difficult to consistently live out because it flies in the face of our created order: "The Lord will fulfill his purpose for me," the psalmist writes, "your steadfast love, O Lord, endures forever." (Psalm 138:8) Likewise, Jeremiah's oft quoted encouragement speaks to a life of significant purpose: "For I know the plans I have for you, declares the Lord, plans for welfare and not for evil, to give you a future and a hope." (Jeremiah 29:11) Despite its practical difficulties however, meaninglessness is the rational conclusion of life without God.

Nihilistic Beginnings and Meaningless Endings

The genealogy of atheism can be traced beyond the Enlightenment to various Roman poets like Lucretius and on to Greek philosophers like Epicurus and Democritus. These men helped develop a philosophy of what was at the time called atomism; this was a nascent form of naturalistic materialism which contributed to the classical world a strong sense of fate and futility regarding human purpose.[70] Millennia later, it was men like Bertrand Russell who, with no small amount of poetic gloom, phrased in more contemporary terms the end result of naturalistic assumptions:

> Man is the product of causes which had no pre-vision of the end they were achieving; that his origin, his growth, his hopes and fears, his loves and his beliefs, are but the outcome of accidental collocations of atoms; that no fire, no heroism, no intensity of thought and feeling, can preserve an individual life beyond the grave; that all the labors of the ages, all the devotion, all the inspiration, all the noonday brightness of human genius, are destined to extinction in the vast death of the solar system, and that the whole temple of Man's achievement must inevitably be buried beneath the debris of a universe in ruins... Only within the scaffolding of these truths, only on the firm foundation of unyielding despair, can the soul's habitation henceforth be safely

---

[70] Guinness, Fool's, 61.

built. [71]

To the evangelical and Biblically oriented ear, sentiments like Russell's above will sound void of hope or celebration. And yet for at least some committed atheists, the silver lining to nihilistic conclusions is appealing. Polish poet Czeslaw Milosz observes how there exists great relief in "a belief in nothingness after death – the huge solace of thinking that for our betrayals, greed, cowardice, murders we are not going to be judged."[72] Atheist author Aldous Huxley spoke with similar candor: "For myself, as, no doubt, for most of my contemporaries, the philosophy of meaninglessness was essentially an instrument of liberation...from a certain system of morality... There was one admirably simple method of...justifying ourselves in our political and erotic revolt: we could deny that the world had any meaning whatsoever."[73]

The Old Testament Scriptures speak often, particularly in the wisdom literature, to this felt sense of nihilism and the absence of justice. Habbakuk for instance, consistent with the later Pauline framework of God's glory actively suppressed, offers an entire book on theodicy. The author of Ecclesiastes also, at the book's conclusion, declares his famous summary statement, "The end of the matter; all has been heard. Fear God and keep his commandments, for this is the whole duty of man. For God will bring every deed into judgment, with every secret thing, whether good or evil."

Bertrand Russell made no secret of his disappointment in the traditional, Christian conceptions of ultimate and eternal justice. Although he found Jesus rather likeable in many ways, he offers this: "There is one very serious defect to my mind in Christ's moral character, and that is that He believed in hell. I do not myself feel that any person who is really profoundly humane can believe in everlasting punishment. Christ certainly as depicted in the Gospels did believe in everlasting punishment, and one does find repeatedly a vindictive fury against those people who would not listen to His preaching."[74] Russell's frustration with Christian conceptions

---

[71] Bertrand Russell, "A Free Man's Worship," 1903, accessed on February 15, 2016, http://www3.nd.edu/~afreddos/courses/264/fmw.htm.

[72] Czelaw Milosz, "The Discreet Charm of Nihilism," *New York Review of Books*, November 19, 1998, accessed on February 15, 2016, http://www.nybooks.com/articles/1998/11/19/discreet-charm-of-nihilism/.

[73] Aldous Huxley, *Ends and Means: An Inquiry into the Nature of Ideals and into the Methods Employed for their Realization* (London: Chatto and Windus, 1941), 273.

[74] Russell, *Christian*, 17.

of the afterlife ring hollow however, when one considers the Biblical God was so intensely against sending individuals to hell – including atheists – that in their place, He went to hell himself.

Despite the "convenience" of choices without eternal consequence, many will still admit the despondency of a worldview committed to no overarching narrative. Atheist cosmologist Lawrence Krauss memorably expressed, "We are a 1% bit of pollution within the universe. We are completely insignificant."[75] Atheist philosopher John Gray states, ""We cannot escape the finality of tragedy... there is no redemption from being human."[76] And Christian author Andy Bannister accurately sums up the situation: "If there is no God...you're alone in a universe that cares as little about you (and your enjoyment) as it does about the fate of the amoeba, the ant, or the aardvark. There's no hope, there's no justice, and there's certainly nothing inherently wrong with poverty, incidentally, so quit protesting."[77]

A Biblical Solution

Stepping into the void of nihilistic anguish, Scripture presents an altogether different picture of reality, one in which humanity is invited into the story of God's glory manifest in all creation. The doctrine of Union with Christ teaches that via one resting by faith in the finished work of Jesus, individuals are offered not only ultimate purpose but temporal care as well. "Therefore I tell you, do not be anxious about your life, what you will eat or what you will drink, nor about your body, what you will put on. Is not life more than food, and the body more than clothing?... Consider the lilies of the field, how they grow: they neither toil nor spin, yet I tell you, even Solomon in all his glory was not arrayed like one of these." (Matthew 6:25-33)

The Christian author J.R.R. Tolkien once penned a short story about a struggling painter named Niggle who spent his entire life trying to create a beautiful picture of a forest vista with mountains in the distance. But Niggle was so desperate to make the picture perfect, he never finished more than a single leaf on a single tree. Endlessly obsessing, he eventually

[75] Amanda Lohrey, "The Big Nothing: Lawrence Krauss and Arse-Kicking Physics", The Monthly, October 2012, accessed on February 15, 2016, https://www.themonthly.com.au/issue/2012/october/1354074365/amanda-lohrey/big-nothing.

[76] John Gray, The Silence of Animals (New York: Farrar, Straus, and Giroux, 2013), 208.

[77] Bannister, Exist, 20.

fell ill and died without completing his work. But as Tolkien relays the story, it was after his death, when Niggle arrived in heaven, that he approached the edge of the heavenly country and saw a tree. In fact, it was *his* tree – finished and complete – every leaf made perfect. Christianity suggests that all humanity can experience this type of fulfillment, portrayed in the Niggle metaphor. Once caught up into God's greater purposes, lives are rendered no longer meaningless but instead woven together into the grand theme of God's redemptive design.[78] "But for this purpose I have raised you up, to show you my power, so that my name may be proclaimed in all the earth." (Exodus 9:16)

Section 6 of 6
V24-25, Identity Suppressed (and idolatry in its place)

The theme of meaninglessness supplanting God's glory feeds into Paul's final point in the Romans 1 pericope – rejection of God leads to suppression of identity with idolatry offered in its place. "Therefore God gave them up in the lusts of their hearts to impurity, to the dishonoring of their bodies among themselves, because they exchanged the truth about God for a lie and worshiped and served the creature rather than the Creator, who is blessed forever! Amen." (Romans 1:24-25)

Inherent Human Dignity

Paul's argument leads the reader to a natural conclusion: those who do not seek identity from a transcendent Creator will eventually settle for grounding identity in creation itself. None other than Charles Darwin, writing to a friend, sensed the danger inherent in this path, "The horrid doubt always arises whether the convictions of man's mind, which has been developed from the mind of the lower animals, are of any value or at all trustworthy."[79] Biblical theology, in contradistinction, teaches that humanity possesses profound value because it is imbued with the very image of God. "On you was I cast from my birth, and from my mother's womb you have been my God." (Psalm 22:10) Michael Perry observes that

---

[78] Timothy Keller and Katherine Leary Alsdorf, *Every Good Endeavor: Connecting Your Work to God's Work* (New York: Dutton, 2012), 24-29.
[79] Timothy Keller, *The Reason for God* (New York: Dutton, 2008), 138.

"ethics, law, and human rights theory are based on the belief that you are not just a random collection of atoms, but a person with dignity and worth."[80]

Violence is done to the concept of human dignity once the creator God is removed from the equation. Many individuals will sense this loss at some level, and thus seek new purpose and meaning in the elevation to idol status of the created order. "To reject God … you must start again with new foundations, explaining why one particular creature thrown up by the blind forces of time and chance churning the primordial soup for billions of years possesses inalienable rights whereas amoebae, cockroaches, and eggplants do not."[81]

Idols Reduce Dignity

The replacement gods that Paul references in verse 25, be they physical idols or merely conceptual ones, ultimately accomplish the very opposite of the atheist's desire which is emancipation of the human mind from the shackles of divine restraint. Emma Goldman optimistically suggests, "Atheism in its negation of gods is at the same time the strongest affirmation of man, and through man, the eternal yea to life, purpose, and beauty."[82] Religion, the atheist believes, is man's demotion.

The problem with Goldman's framework is that idolatry always leads to a lower view of human life, not a higher one. When a worldview exchanges the Creator for something instead created, inherent in the substitution is the replacement of humanity made in God's image for humanity made in the image of – something else. The history of philosophy is to a striking degree one of setting up intentional God surrogates. Literary critic Terry Eagleton identifies several modern day idols: Enlightenment rationalists make a god of reason; Romantics deify the imagination; nationalists idealize the nation; Marxists offer an economic version of sin and salvation. "Not believing in God is a far more arduous affair than is generally imagined."[83]

Earlier in the Romans 1 passage, the author makes the charge that in seeking wisdom, the one who rejects God for replacement idols has

---

[80] Michael J. Perry, "The Morality of Human Rights: A Nonreligious Ground?," *Emory Law Journal,* 54, 2005, 97-150.

[81] Banniser, *Exist,* 39.

[82] Goldman, *Portable,* 133.

[83] Terry Eagleton, *Culture and the Death of God* (New Haven, CT: Yale University Press, 2014), 119.

inadvertently embraced foolishness. The root word for foolish, *syniemi*, means to synthesize, to put things together into the mind. To be foolish therefore is to fail to connect ideas or link them into a meaningful structure. Lacking coherency, worldview and sense of identity becomes internally contradictory, fragmented, and fractured.[84] This loss of coherent identity is the end-result of atheism, which detaches itself from something greater than itself. Stephen Prothero of Boston University recognizes that replacement belief becomes a new creed entirely. "Atheism is a religion of sorts, or can be. Many atheists are quite religious, holding their views about God with the conviction of zealots and evangelizing with verve… It stands at the center of their lives, defining who they are, how they think, and with whom they associate. The question of God is never far from their minds."[85]

Redemption Restores Dignity

Humanity's identity, as creatures bearing the fingerprints of God, is entirely bound up in the nature of God and His stated redemptive purpose in creation. For those who believe, this will offer hope and freedom that refreshes the soul. For those who reject a personal God, the Biblical story of redemption can only offer frustration and condescension.

It is not at all difficult to see what it is about such a God that turns otherwise pleasant things distasteful. When a concrete, personal God takes the helm, mere submission sinks into worship. Favor boomerangs into gratitude. Death transforms from the finish line of a few decades to the threshold of eternity. Faith sobers from tentative confidence to total commitment. Guilt becomes repentance. Rules become commandments. Mere punishment swells into judgment. Detached pardon descends to in-the-flesh redemption. While hell rages into the great divorce, heaven climaxes into the wedding of the Lamb. The problem of moral evil hardens into rebellion. In the end, each life becomes a battleground of eternal possibility.[86]

---

[84] Pearcey, *Truth*, 163.

[85] Stephen Prothero, *God is Not the One: The Eight Rival Religions That Run the World* (New York: HarperOne, 2010), 326.

[86] Geisler, *Flaw*, 148.

Introduction

Edmund Burke once said, "Boldness formerly was not the character of atheists as such. They were even of a character nearly the reverse; they were formerly like the old Epicureans, rather an unenterprising race. But of late they are grown active, designing, turbulent and seditious."[1] This quote is from the eighteenth century, but may rightly be appropriated for the twenty-first-century's rise of New Atheism. In the year 2016, and for the decade prior, the volume of present-day atheism has been steadily increasing.

Atheism likely originated in ancient Greece, although it did not emerge as an overt belief system until much later during the Enlightenment. It was during the Enlightenment that a systematic attempt was developed to present and promulgate a godless worldview as an alternative to a religious one. During this era, Atheism sought to take ideals like the rejection of superstition, hierarchy, and rationally undergirded authority to what atheist Julian Baggini, in *Atheism: A Very Short Introduction*, suggests is a logical conclusion: "It certainly fits atheism's self-image to say that, once

---

[1] Paul Rahe, *Republics Ancient and Modern: Classical Republicanism and the American Revolution* (Chapel Hill: University of North Carolina Press, 1992), 233.

69

we were prepared to look religion in the eye under the cool light of reason, its untruth became self-evident. It just obviously was superstition and myth, grounded not in the divine but in particular, local human practices."[2]

In the current chapter, the goal will be to consider the current ethos of atheism by placing contemporary atheists into "conversation" with one another; particular emphasis will be placed upon the writings of militant New Atheists like Richard Dawkins, Daniel Dennett, Sam Harris, Christopher Hitchens, and Lawrence Krauss. An array of topics and emphases can be identified within the scope of these authors. However, across the work of New Atheism, two "evolutions" and five themes are elucidated time and time again to form the core of New Atheism doctrine. It is to these seven categories we now turn our attention:

1. Religion as Cultural Evolution
2. Religion as Biological Evolution
3. Naturalism
4. Scientism
5. Moralism
6. Rationalism
7. Nihilism

Section 1 of 7
Religion as Cultural Evolution

Religion and its Study

Daniel Dennett, professor of philosophy at Tufts University, has completed the most widely known work positioning religion as a mere byproduct of cultural evolution. Rejecting all forms of supernaturalism, Dennett views his work as analogous to a cell phone suddenly ringing at a concert where the listener has become awestruck and breathless, carried away by the music. Suddenly, because of the ring-tone intrusion, the spell is broken and reality rushes back in. Dennett suggests in *Breaking the Spell*:

> *It is high time that we subject religion as a global phenomenon to the most intensive multidisciplinary research we can muster, calling on the best minds on the planet. Why? Because religion is too important for us to remain ignorant about. It affects not just our*

---

[2] Julian Baggini, *Atheism: A Very Short Introduction*, (New York: Oxford University Press, 2003), 80.

social, political, and economic conflicts, but the very meanings we find in our lives. For many people, probably a majority of the people on Earth, nothing matters more than religion.[3]

If religion is defined as social systems whose participants avow belief in a supernatural agent or agents who approval is to be sought, there exists within New Atheism a desire to quantify and explain the cultural developments by which religious conviction has come about. Dismissed from the outset is any real possibility of supernatural intervention. Instead, the accusation is levied that there exists an asymmetry: "Atheists in general welcome the most intensive and objective examination of their views, practices, and reasons... The religious, in contrast, often bristle at the impertinence, the lack of respect, the *sacrilege*, implied by anybody who wants to investigate their views... *This* spell must be broken, and broken now."[4]

Someone once said that "Philosophy is questions that may never be answered. Religion is answers that may never be questioned." To whatever extent this ethos is true of Christianity in general and evangelicalism in particular, times must change. In a social media age that breeds skepticism and suspicion, Christians must be seen as altogether willing to subject their beliefs to scientific and intellectual rigor. If Biblical truth is truth indeed, it can and will withstand the test.

Religion and Its Development

Marcel Gauchet begins his book on the political history of religion by noting, almost in passing, "As far as we know, religion has without exception existed at all times and in all places."[5] Dennett sharply disagrees, however, dismissing the "pinched perspective" of a historian and asserting otherwise. "There was a time before religious beliefs and practices had occurred to anyone. There was a time, after all, before there were any *believers* on the planet, before there were any beliefs about anything."[6] It is not immediately clear what evidence Dennett possesses for a once-upon-a-time, complete absence of religion. In contrast, anthropologist Anthony Wallace estimates that in the past 10,000 years, humans have constructed

---

[3] Daniel C. Dennett, *Breaking the Spell: Religion as a Natural Phenomenon* (New York: The Penguin Group, 2006), 14-15.

[4] Dennett, *Spell*, 17.

[5] Marcel Gauchet, *The Disenchantment of the World: A Political History of Religion* (Princeton NJ: Princeton University Press, 1997), 22.

[6] Dennett, *Spell*, 98.

no less than 100,000 religions. "Most people believe in a god of some kind, and if the historians, anthropologists, and archaeologists are right, almost everyone who ever lived believed in one god or another."[7]

Beginning with vehement argument against the ubiquity of religious conviction in ancient history, Dennett develops his thesis that out of the vacuum of religious belief, Folk Religion developed *ex nihilo*. "Folk religion," over and against "organized religion," differs markedly in this schema, for Folk Religion's practitioners don't think of themselves as *practicing* a religion at all. Religious practice, instead, is a seamless part of the individual's lives. "One way to tell that they really believe in the deities to which they make their sacrifices is that they aren't forever talking about how much they believe in their deities – any more than you and I go around assuring each other that we believe in germs and atoms."[8]

Out of Folk Religion, as the theory goes, organized religion developed in much the same way that folk music spawned organized music. "As people became more and more reflective about both their practices and their reactions, they could then become more and more inventive in their explorations of the pace of possibilities. Both music and religion gradually became more "artful" or sophisticated, more elaborate, more of a production."[9]

Following folk religion and organized religion, the third and final step in the atheist's understanding of the cultural evolution of faith-based belief is contemporary religion, or what Dennett refers to as "belief in belief."

> In religion...the experts are not exaggerating for effect when they say they don't understand what they are talking about. The fundamental incomprehensibility of God is insisted upon as a central tenet of faith... why does anybody go along with this? The answer is obvious: belief in belief. Many people believe in God. Many people believe in belief in God. What's the difference? People who believe in God are sure that God exists, and they are glad, because they hold God to be the most wonderful of all things. People who moreover believe in belief in God are sure that belief in God exists...and they think that this is a good state of affairs, something to be strongly encouraged and fostered wherever

---

[7] Michael Shermer, *How We Believe: Science, Skepticism, and the Search for God* (New York: Holt Paperbacks, 2000), 140.

[8] Dennett, *Spell*, 160-161.

[9] Dennett, *Spell*, 153.

possible... It is entirely possible to be an atheist and believe in belief in God. Such a person doesn't believe in God but nevertheless thinks that believing in God would be a wonderful state of mind to be in.

Contemporary religion then, particularly with respect to the American context, is an amalgam of true religious conviction coupled with a tolerance of religious faith because of its mostly harmless and occasionally helpful effects. This *belief in belief* approach is evidenced, for instance, in the booming phenomenon of mega churches which go out of their way to give members plenty of elbow room for personal, Scriptural interpretation. Author Alan Wolfe distinguishes sharply between modern evangelicalism and fundamentalism, "which tends to be more preoccupied with matters of theological substance... Evangelicalism's popularity is due as much to its populistic and democratic urges — its determination to find out exactly what believers want and to offer it to them — as it is to certainties of the faith."[10] For the committed, Gospel-centered Christian, these observations will be sobering.

New Atheism is at times perplexed by the evolution of religious conviction running parallel to an increase of education in the communication age. "While most developed societies have grown predominantly secular, with the curious exception of the United States, orthodox religion is in florid bloom throughout the developing world. In fact, humanity seems to be growing proportionally *more* religious, as prosperous, nonreligious people have the fewest babies."[11] At the beginning of the twentieth century, social scientists predicted that with the advent of universal public education and the rise of science and technology, culture would become secularized and religiosity would dramatically decrease.[12] Indeed, Dennett's explicit, hoped-for vision of the future is one in which religion is almost entirely marginalized from cultural as an impacting force.

> *Religion diminishes in prestige and visibility, rather like smoking; it is tolerated, since there are those who say they can't live without it, but it is discouraged, and teaching religion to impressionable young children is frowned upon in most societies and actually outlawed in*

---

[10] Alan Wolfe, *The Transformation of American Religion: How We Actually Live Our Faith* (New York: Free Press, 2003), 361.

[11] Sam Harris, *The Moral Landscape: How Science Can Determine Human Values* (Free Press: New York, NY), 2010.

[12] Shermer, *Believe*, 22.

others. In this scenario, politicians who still practice religion can be elected if they prove themselves worthy in other regards, but few would advertise their religious affiliation – or affliction, as the politically incorrect insist on calling it. It is considered as rude to draw attention to the religion of somebody as it is to comment in public about his sexuality or whether she has been divorced.[13]

Religion and its Propagation

In the Darwinian, evolutionary model, natural selection is the theory posited to explain the genetic promulgation of mutated features across generations in an organism. Similarly, New Atheism is eager to devise a workable, naturalistic theory that explains the cultural transmission of *religious* features. Bertrand Russell, for instance, the twentieth-century forerunner of New Atheism, believed that "what really moves people to believe in God is not any intellectual argument at all. Most people believe in God because they have been taught from early infancy to do it, and that is the main reason."[14]

A popular theory among the new atheists, first posited by Richard Dawkins in his 1970's work, *The Selfish Gene*, is the idea of memes, or small packets of culturally transmitted information.[15] The overall concept is explained more recently by Dennett, using an illustration from the world of entomology:

> *You watch an ant in a meadow, laboriously climbing up a blade of grass, higher and higher until it falls... No biological benefit accrues to the ant... Its brain has been commandeered by a tiny parasite, a lancet flute (Discrocelium dendriticum), that needs to get itself into the stomach of a sheep or a cow in order to complete its reproductive cycle. This little brain worm is driving the ant into position to benefit its progeny, not the ant's. Does anything like this ever happen with human beings? Yes, indeed. We often find human beings setting aside their personal interests, their health, their chances to have children, and devoting their entire lives to furthering the interests of an idea that has lodged in their brains.[16]*

---

[13] Dennett, *Spell*, 36.

[14] Bertrand Russell, *Why I Am Not a Christian: and other essays on religion and related subjects* (New York: Simon & Schuster, Inc., 1957), 14.

[15] Richard Dawkins, *The Selfish Gene* (New York: Oxford University Press, 2006).

The theory is that at least one, and perhaps both, parties in the religious-individual/religious-belief partnership must benefit. David Sloan Wilson, author of *Darwin's Cathedral*, argues a hypothesis that religion is a social phenomenon designed by evolution to improve cooperation within human groups.[17] It stands to reason that in a cultural environment where ideas compete, those ideas that encourage people to act together will spread more effectively. Thus religion becomes a means of unification within (although obviously not among) human groups. Dawkins's and Dennett's spin is slightly less positive than Sloan's, implying the wild memes of folk religion are like rats, squirrels, pigeons, and cold viruses in that they are adapted to living with, and at times exploiting, humans.

> *The boat builders and boat owners no more need to understand the reasons why their boats are symmetrical than the fruit-eating bear needs to understand his role in propagating wild apple trees when he defecates in the woods. Here we have the design of a human artifact – culturally, not genetically transmitted – without a human designer, without an author or inventor or even a knowing editor or critic.*[18]

In the end, the new Atheist's conviction is that religion, a culturally transmitted idea, is an idea that needs to *stop* transmitting. "I think all the great religions of the world," Russell wrote, "Buddhism, Hinduism, Christianity, Islam, and Communism – both untrue and harmful."[19] Dawkins views religion at best as a childish myth: "Father Christmas and the Tooth Fairy are part of the charm of childhood. So is God. Some of us grow out of all three."[20] Dennett, however, puts as fine a point on the topic as any:

> *We've got ourselves caught in a hypocrisy trap, and there is no clear path out. Are we like the families in which the adults go through all the motions of believing in Santa Claus for the sake of the kids, and the kids all pretend still to believe in Santa Claus so as not to spoil the adults' fun? If only our current predicament were as innocuous and even comical as that! In the adult world of religion, people are dying and killing, with the moderates cowed into silence by the intransigence of the radicals in their own faiths, and many*

---

[16] Dennett, *Spell*, 3-4.
[17] David Sloan Wilson, *Darwin's Cathedral: Evolution, Religion, and the Nature of Society* (Chicago: University of Chicago Press, 2002).
[18] Dennett, *Spell*, 78.
[19] Russell, *Christian*, v.
[20] *Third Way* magazine, Vol. 26, No. 5, June 2003, p.5.

afraid to acknowledge what they actually believe for fear of breaking Granny's heart.[21]

Section 2 of 7
Religion as Biological Evolution

Belief in the Brain

In the atheist's search to explain transmission of religious belief, the source of inquiry considered above is religion as *cultural* evolution. The second form of inquiry is religion as *biological* evolution. What neurological or genetic factors, asks the atheist, may be in play when it comes to supernatural belief? Sam Harris, the Stanford educated philosopher and neuroscientist, suggests:

> *Introspection offers no clue that our experience of the world around us, and of ourselves within it, depends upon voltage changes and chemical interactions taking place in our heads. And yet a century and a half of brain science declares it to be so... With respect to our current scientific understanding of the mind, the major religions remain wedded to doctrines that are growing less plausible by the day.*[22]

Humans evolved, so the theory goes, to be skilled, pattern-seeking creatures. Individuals most effective at identifying patterns (for instance, standing upwind of animals is detrimental to the hunt, cow manure is an effective aid for crop-growing) tended to leave behind the most offspring. However, the skill of finding patterns is only half the battle – identifying which patterns are meaningful and which are not is a separate ability and the human brain is not always effective at identifying the difference. This failure is due to the fact that identifying meaningless patterns will often do no harm and actually may do some good by reducing anxiety in uncertain environments. So the mammalian, pattern-finding brain, becomes an evolved, religion-*creating* brain by embracing two separate pattern errors: #1, believing a falsehood; #2, rejecting a truth.[23]

Because of its presuppositional dismissal of supernaturalism, New Atheism is curious which biological factors might account for the

---

[21] Dennett, *Spell*, 291.
[22] Harris, *Landscape*, 158.
[23] Shermer, *Believe*, 38.

persistence of religious belief. Dennett suggests, "Karl Marx may have been more right than he knew when he called religion the opiate of the masses. Might we have a god center in our brains along with our sweet tooth?"[24] Richard Dawkins states, "If neuroscientists find a 'god center' in the brain, Darwinian scientists like me want to know why the god center evolved. Why did those of our ancestors who had a genetic tendency to grow a god center survive better than rivals who did not?"[25]

Michael Shermer, self-labeled agnostic and founding publisher of Skeptic magazine, offers something of a theory to answer Dawkins's question. Shermer coined the term "Belief Engine" to explain the genetically derived tendency to identify patterns, seek causal relationships, and occasionally process intellectual mistakes that lead to religious belief. The reason these environmental, interpretive mistakes continue to propagate, in Shermer's paradigm, is that the belief engine remains a useful mechanism for survival. Psychological evidence suggests "magical thinking" can reduce anxiety in uncertain environments. Medical evidence suggests prayer, meditation, and worship across religious convictions can lead to greater physical and mental health.[26] The religious confusion, therefore, together with the personal benefits, live on.

Belief in the Genes

If neurological origins compose one half of the atheist's religious transmission theory, genetic origins form the second half. Over a century before the rise of New Atheism, William James speculated that although not true of everyone, he himself possessed a brute need for religion: "Call this, if you like, my mystical *germ*. It is a very common germ. It creates the rank and file of believers. And it withstands in my case, so it will withstand in most cases, all purely, atheistic criticism."[27] Dennett picks up on this hypothesis and wonders if there exists a genetic variation in religious sensitivity, analogous to the genetic variation among humans in taste and olfaction.[28]

---

[24] Dennett, Spell, 14.

[25] Richard Dawkins, "What Use is Religion? Part 1", Free Inquiry, June/July, accessed June 14, 2016, http://www.beliefnet.com/news/2001/04/what-good-is-religion.aspx.

[26] Shermer, *Believe*, 38.

[27] William James, *The Varieties of Religious Experience* (New York: Penguin, 1982), xxiv.

[28] Dennett, Spell, 83.

The famous Minnesota twins study, which examined the nature versus nurture question on a number of variables in twins separated at birth, considered closely the question of religiosity. Researchers found that religious correlations between identical twins were typically double those of fraternal twins, "'suggesting that genetic factors play a significant role in the expression of this trait.' The twin study experts concluded: 'Social scientists will have to discard the *a priori* assumption that individual differences in religious and other social attitudes are solely influenced by environmental factors.'"[29] Dennett pushes this hypothesis to its furthest degree:

> We could consider the parallel with the genetic differences that help to account for some Asians' and some Native Americans' difficulty with alcohol. As with variation in lactose tolerance, there is genetically transmitted variation in the ability to metabolize alcohol, due to variation in the presence of enzymes, mainly alcohol dehydrogenase and aldehyde dehydrogenase. Needless to say, since, through no fault of their own, alcohol is poisonous to people with these genes – or it turns them into alcoholics... Might there be either "spiritual experience intolerance" or "spiritual-experience distaste?"[30]

In the late 1990's, University of California neuroscientist Dr. Vilaynur Ramachandran delivered a paper at the annual meeting of The Society for Neuroscience which he titled "The Neural Basis of Religious Experience." In his presentation, Ramachandran argued that an individual's preference for religion or lack thereof may depend on how enhanced a part of the brain's electrical circuity becomes. "If these preliminary results hold up, they may indicate that the neural substrate for religion and belief in God may partially involve circuitry in the temporal lobes, which is enhanced in some patients."[31]   According to neuroscientist David Noelle, however, the hypothesis that neural mechanisms underlying religion form a distinct brain module was not really tested by these experiments. He concluded that reports of evidence for a 'God module' in the brain or at the genetic level are, at best, premature. Instead, a "reasonable hypothesis is that the handful of fanatic religious leaders throughout history, who report...communicating with God, the devil, angels, aliens and other

---

[29] Shermer, *Believe*, 64.
[30] Dennett, *Spell*, 317-318.
[31] Shermer, *Believe*, 65.

supernatural beings, can perhaps be accounted for by temporal lobe abnormalities and anomalies."

Ultimately, a neurological or genetic sensitivity to religious belief remains an open question, yet completely misses the point of whether religion in general, or Christianity in particular, is actually true. Baggini's mind is made up, however, and is representative of contemporary atheistic thought on the matter:

> *You can choose between the atheist hypothesis that consciousness is a product of brain activity or an implausible tale about how non-material thinking souls exist alongside brains and somehow interact with them, and that, further, the dependency of consciousness on brain activity miraculously disappears at death, when the soul lives on without the body.*[32]

Section 3 of 7
Naturalism

Across the spectrum of New Atheist doctrine, the evolution of religion due to both cultural and biological factors, rather than actual experience of the divine, is accepted as a given. Beyond religious evolution, five additional factors form the core of New Atheism dogma. The first of these five factors is a commitment to philosophical naturalism.

Materialism Minimizes Religion

Most atheists are physicalists in at least one general sense: their atheism is motivated in part by their naturalism, the belief that only the natural world exists and the *super*natural is myth. This conviction means that the only kind of stuff that can exist is physical stuff. There are no non-physical souls, spirits, or even ideas.[33] Naturalistic implications are far-reaching; when it comes to the realm of religious belief, naturalism is inextricably tied to the previously considered topics of religion's cultural and biological evolution. If no extra-normal realm exists, religion will always suffer as reductionism. That is to say, within a naturalistic framework, religion can only be viewed as a human phenomenon

---

[32] Baggini, *Introduction*, 30.
[33] Baggini, *Introduction*, 4-5.

composed of events, organisms, objects, structures, patterns and the like that all obey the laws of physics or biology and do not – ever – involve actual miracles.[34] Some phenomena will remain unexplained, of course, but the atheist posits that once an explanation does finally come along, the explanation will always be naturalistic.[35]

Methodology for the outright dismissal of all supernatural explanation varies widely. Lawrence Krauss, theoretical physicist and cosmologist is both honest and representative of the New Atheist position: "In the interests of full disclosure right at the outset I must admit that I am not sympathetic to the conviction that creation requires a creator, which is at the basis of all of the world's religions."[36] Dennett expresses frustration when either the God of the Bible, or an intelligent designer in general, do not conform to his standards of humility: "I know professors who can get mighty annoyed if you pretend you haven't heard of their published work, but it is hard to see why the Creative Intelligence that invented DNA and the metabolic cycle and mangrove trees and sperm whales would care whether any of Its creatures recognized its authorship."[37] Dennett's solution, given the dissonance between a supernatural god and said god's faith requirements, is to dismiss the concept altogether. Dennett perceives, however, no cultural or moral loss at stake:

> There is no reason at all why a disbelief in the immateriality or immortality of the soul should make a person less caring, less moral, less committed to the well-being of everybody on Earth than somebody who believes in "the spirit." … A good scientific materialist can be just as concerned about whether there is plenty of justice, love, joy, beauty, political freedom, and, yes, even religious freedom as about whether there is plenty of food and clothing, for instance, since all of these are material benefits, and some are more important than others.[38]

Materialism Masks Teleology (Design)

In the 2009 documentary *Collision*, which followed a series of debates between evangelical theologian Douglas Wilson and militant New Atheist

---

[34] Dennett, *Spell*, 23.

[35] Baggini, *Introduction*, 27.

[36] Lawrence Krauss. *A Universe From Nothing: Why There is Something Rather Than Nothing* (New York: Atria Paperback, 2012), xxi.

[37] Dennett, *Spell*, 265.

[38] Dennett, *Spell*, 305.

Christopher Hitchens, a surprising admission was captured from the latter: "At some point, certainly, we [atheists] are all asked which is the best argument you come up against from the other side. I think every one of us picks the fine-tuning one as the most intriguing… You have to spend time thinking about it, working on it. It's not trivial."[39]   Hitchens uncharacteristically admits an intellectual hurdle multiple believers have struggled to reconcile as well: *how can a purely naturalistic universe with no outside designer display such striking evidence of design?* Antony Flew, the devout, atheist philosopher who ultimately embraced theism, shares the confusion: "This, too, is my conclusion. The only satisfactory explanation for the origin of such 'end-directed, self-replicating' life as we see on earth is an infinitely intelligent Mind."[40]

Despite the myriad of both religious and non-religious scientists who admit the appearance of design in nature, it should not be assumed that this is a convincing point of discussion for atheists in general. Says Russell:

> When you come to look into this argument from design, it is a most astonishing thing that people can believe that this world, with all the things that are in it, with all its defects, should be the best that omnipotence and omniscience have been able to produce in millions of years. I really cannot believe it. Do you think that, if you were granted omnipotence and omniscience and millions of years in which to perfect your world, you could produce nothing better than the Ku Klux Klan or the Fascists?[41]

Krauss, likewise, is eager to offer naturalistic rationale for the seeming design of nature without providing room for the supernatural. He admits that two different conclusions may be drawn from a teleological consideration of the material world. The first potential conclusion, drawn by Isaac Newton, Galileo, and a host of other scientists over the years, concluded that order is the creation of divine intelligence. The second potential conclusion is that instead, the laws of physics themselves are all that exist. These laws do not merely allow for the existence of the universe, but in fact require it to both develop and evolve. Humanity, then, becomes an irrevocable by-product of said physical laws.[42]

---

[39] Darren Doane, "Collision," accessed on April 11, 2015, https://www.youtube.com/watch?v=cCUmKP4NFKs.

[40] Flew, *Notorious*, 132.

[41] Russell, *Christian*, 10.

[42] Krauss, *Nothing*, 142.

The fundamental constants of nature, so long assumed to take on special importance, may just be environmental accidents. If we scientists tend to take ourselves and our science too seriously, maybe we also have taken our universe too seriously... Maybe our universe is rather like a tear buried in a vast, multiversal ocean of possibilities.[43]

From the Christian perspective, the end result of naturalism is an existence in which humanity as image-bearers of God is devalued and diminished. In Baggini's worldview, however, "[W]hatever people are, they are first and foremost mortal creatures who do not have immortal, spiritual souls... Consciousness is a product of brain activity and with no brain, there is no consciousness. In fact, this is so startlingly obvious that it is astonishing that anyone can really doubt it."[44]

Perhaps the most striking implication of a naturalistic worldview is that the design apparent in an individual's own thoughts – that is, his *own* design – becomes also a mere mirage. While an individual continually notices changes in his own experience – thought, mood, perception, behavior, etc – he is ultimately unaware of the neural events that produce these experiences. Because consciousness cannot be explained outside a materialistic understanding, all thoughts and behavior are traced back to biological and neurological events which the individual has no conscious knowledge of. Ultimately thoughts and intentions, then, are caused by physical events and mental stirrings of which no one is actually aware. This philosophy becomes the basis for New Atheist Sam Harris's assertion that free will itself is nothing more than an illusion.

The phrase "free will" describes what it feels like to be identified with the content of each thought as it arises in consciousness... But from a deeper perspective (speaking both subjectively and objectively), thoughts simply arise (what else could they do?) unauthored and yet author to our actions.[45]

Materialism Motivates Cosmology (Origin)

One of the greatest challenges to an atheistic, naturalistic view of reality is the cosmological problem – why is there something when there

---

[43] Krauss, *Nothing*, 138.

[44] Baggini, *Introduction*, 18.

[45] Sam Harris, *The Moral Landscape: How Science Can Determine Human Values* (New York: Free Press, 2010), 105.

ought to be nothing? Or phrased a different way – what is the cause of the universe? Antony Flew, the vehement atheist turned theist wrote his two, main anti-theological works before the development of big bang cosmology or the introduction of the fine-tuning argument from physical constants. But beginning in the early 1980's, because of scientific discovery, Flew began the long process of reconsidering his positions. Later he confessed, "Atheists have to be embarrassed by the contemporary cosmological consensus, for it seemed that the cosmologists were providing a scientific proof of what St. Thomas Aquinas contended could not be proved philosophically; namely, that the universe had a beginning."[46] Of course, in the mind of the atheist the universe having a beginning, and that beginning being *God*, are surely not one and the same. Into the twentieth century, it should be understood the popular view was one of an eternally existent universe. Russell, for instance, wrote in the late nineteen twenties, "There is no reason why the world...should not have always existed... The idea that things must have a beginning is really due to the poverty of our imagination."[47] The dawn of modern cosmology presented a new, theoretical wrinkle by introducing the question of universal origin. This question became one of the primary factors that led to Flew's intellectual embrace of a divine creator.

Theoretical physicist Lawrence Krauss counters the theist's cosmological position; he points out that declaration of a first cause still leaves open the question "who created the creator?"

> The central problem with the notion of creation is that it appears to require some externality, something outside of the system itself, to preexist, in order to create the conditions necessary for the system to come into being. This is usually where the notion of God – some external agency existing separate from space, time, and indeed from physical reality itself – comes in, because the buck seems to be required to stop somewhere. But in this sense God seems to me to be a rather facile semantic solution to the deep question of creation.[48]

Krauss recognizes that one can view big bang cosmology as suggestive of a creator, or one can instead choose (as he does) to argue that the

---

[46] Flew, Antony. *There is ~~No~~ A God: How the world's most notorious atheist changed his mind* (New York: HarperCollins Publishers, 2007), 135.

[47] Russell, *Christian*, 7.

[48] Krauss, *Nothing*, 171.

mathematics of general relativity explain the origin of the universe back to its beginning without the intervention of deity. It is here that Krauss introduces his theory which seems to delight atheists while leaving theists scratching their heads. "The structures we can see, like stars and galaxies, were all created by quantum fluctuations from nothing."[49] What exactly are these "quantum fluctuations?" it's never made entirely clear but atheists and agnostics alike appear pleased with their dismissal of God as the necessary causative agent.

> The Hubble Telescope...reveals as never before the rich density of galaxies in our neck of the universe, as grand a statement about the sacred as any medieval cathedral. How vast is the cosmos. How contingent is our place. Yet out of this apparent insignificance emerges a glorious contingency – the recognition that we did not have to be, but here we are.[50]

In addition to cosmological origins, the atheist is further challenged by the problem of biogenesis, the beginning of the chemistry of life. Yet life is more than just complex chemical reactions that require an origin. As any high school biology student can attest, the biological cell is an information processing and replicating system. Paul Davies identifies the difficulty: "The problem of how meaningful or semantic information can emerge spontaneously from a collection of mindless molecules subject to blind and purposeless forces presents a deep conceptual challenge."[51] Nobel prize-winning physiologist George Wald once famously argued, "We choose to believe the impossible: that life arose spontaneously by chance." However, Wald ultimately concluded that a preexisting mind, which he described as the matrix of physical reality, composed a physical universe that could give rise to life.[52]

The question of something from nothing has remained a massive problem for atheism. For this reason, a truly valid theory of cosmological origins could strike a mortal blow to theistic positions. Krauss's much fawned-over three step explanation, quoted in summary form below, should be read slowly and considered carefully.

---

[49] Krauss, *Nothing*, 105.

[50] Shermer, *Believe*, 237.

[51] Paul Davies, "The Origin of Life II: How Did It Begin?" http://aca.mq.edu.au/ PaulDavies/ publications/papers/OriginsOfLife_II.pdf.

[52] George Wald, "Life and Mind in the Universe," in *Cosmos, Bios, Theos*, ed. Henry Margenau and Roy Abraham Varghese (La Salle, IL: Open Court, 1992), 218.

1. **Quantum Fluctuations:** "Small-density fluctuations in empty space due to the rules of quantum mechanics will later be responsible for all the structure we observe in the universe today. So we, and everything we see, result out of quantum fluctuations in what is essentially nothingness near the beginning of time, namely during the inflationary expansion."[53]
2. **Unstable Nothing:** "Quantum gravity not only appears to allow universes to be created from nothing – meaning, in this case, I emphasize, the absence of space and time – it may require them. "Nothing" – in this case no space, no time, no anything! – *is* unstable."[54]
3. **Multiple Universes:** "A multiverse, either in the form of a landscape of universes existing in a host of extra dimensions, or in the form of a possibly infinitely replicating set of universes in a three-dimensional space as in the case of eternal inflation, changes the playing field when we think about the creation of our own universe and the conditions that may be required for that to happen... The question of what determined the laws of nature that allowed our universe to form and evolve now becomes less significant... we would be guaranteed, in such a picture, that some universe would arise with the laws that we have discovered. No mechanism and no entity is required to fix the laws of nature to be what they are."[55]

In the end, the reader is left to consider the case: Does Krauss's three pronged explanation for something from nothing (quantum fluctuations, unstable "nothing," and multiverses) seem convincing? If the theory above seems more reasonable and/or believable than a divine creator, let the reader take note: the implications are disappointing even to Krauss. "Why is there something rather than nothing? Ultimately, this question may be no more significant or profound than asking why some flowers are red and some are blue. 'Something' may always come from nothing. It may be required, independent of the underlying nature of reality."[56]

---

[53] Krauss, *Nothing*, 151.
[54] Krauss, *Nothing*, 170.
[55] Krauss, *Nothing*, 176.
[56] Krauss, *Nothing*, 178.

Science (not Religion) Deserves Ultimate Confidence

If the question of cosmological origins remains the atheist's greatest hurdle, then confidence in Science remains the atheist's greatest hope. Across the work of New Atheism, an optimistic, awe-filled, almost-worship-like attitude is directed toward the scientific endeavor. With reference to the previous section's review of Krauss's "nothing from nothing" cosmology, none other than Richard Dawkins venerates his theory with breathless enthusiasm:

> We can read Lawrence Krauss for what looks to me like the knockout blow. Even the last remaining trump card of the theologian, "Why is there something rather than nothing?" shrivels up before your eyes as you read these pages. If On the Origin of Species was biology's deadliest blow to supernaturalism, we may come to see A Universe from Nothing as the equivalent from cosmology. The title means exactly what it says. And what it says is devastating.[57]

Consistent with Krauss and Dawkins, Dennett agrees a large gulf exists between religious faith and scientific confidence. What has driven the changes in concepts from physics, in his view, is not just heightened skepticism from an increasingly sophisticated audience, but a tidal wave of scientific evidence.[58] Likewise, physicist Steven Weinberg emphasizes that "science does not make it *impossible* to believe in God, but rather makes it possible to *not* believe in God. Without science, everything is a miracle. With science, there remains the possibility that nothing is. Religious belief in this case becomes less and less necessary, and also less and less relevant."[59]

With respect to the topic at hand, one of the most significant developments in contemporary American culture is the impact that scientism (i.e. faith in science) is having beyond the New Atheist dialogue. The public consciousness is increasingly inclined to trade divine authority for hope in science to right society's ills. "Just fifty years ago, in spite of the

---

[57] Richard Dawkin's afterward from Krauss, *Nothing*, 191.
[58] Dennett, *Spell*, 233.
[59] Krauss, *Nothing*, 183.

great advances of physics in the previous half century, we understood only one of the four fundamental forces of nature... In just one subsequent decade, however, not only had three of the four known forces surrendered to our investigations, but a new elegant unity of nature had been uncovered."[60] Note the "surrendered to our investigations" vocabulary; Krauss, like many of the New Atheists is girded by the power of science, and delighted in mankind's use of it. Fewer and fewer sound the alarm of non-theist Michael Shermer:

> The notion that religion will soon fall into disuse would seem to belie the data of both science and anecdotal observation... While scientists may manifest commendable moral traits, or act with admirable social consciousness, they do so as an expression of their humanity, not their science. Science never trafficked, and likely never will, in the business of moral courage and nobility of spirit.[61]

Science (not God) Answers Ultimate Questions

Among the so-called four horsemen of New Atheism (Dawkins, Dennett, Harris, and Hitchens), Sam Harris speaks most often of the hope that science can and will go beyond its traditionally understood sphere of physical observation and also answer the most significant questions of life. "I am arguing that science can, in principle, help us understand what we should do and should want – and, therefore, what other people should do and should want in order to live the best lives possible."[62] If this seems overly optimistic, Harris would counter that some of today's sciences yet remain in their infancy. He sees virtually no ceiling to their reach:

> The neuroscience of morality and social emotions is only just beginning, but there seems no question that it will one day deliver morally relevant insights regarding the material causes of our happiness and suffering... there is every reason to expect that kindness, compassion, fairness, and other classically "good" traits will be vindicated neuroscientifically.[63]

In the wake of a broken world, it is understandable that a godless position would desire some measure of hope. Poverty, injustice, addictions – it is appealing to imagine the scientific endeavor, invented by humanity

---

[60] Krauss, *Nothing*, xviii.
[61] Shermer, *Believe*, 141.
[62] Harris, *Landscape*, 28.
[63] Harris, *Landscape*, 80.

and controlled by mankind, will one day provide ultimate solutions. Again, it is non-Christian, non-theist Michael Shermer who suggests a moment of pause for the science-will-right-all-wrongs drumbeat. "Sometimes we go beyond what our science can really say about some of the great and enduring questions traditionally addressed by religion, particularly the big three... 'Who am I? Where have I come from and where am I going? What is there after this life?'"[64]

Science (not Faith) rooted in Ultimate Reality

Although intellectual, religious believers will argue that atheistic concepts – just like religious ones – require steps of faith, New Atheism disagrees. The real fault line between faith positions and ordinary beliefs, in their framework, is not *proof* but beliefs that accord with evidence, experience, or logic.[65] Therefore, as the thinking goes, atheism is not a faith position. Russell, a significant forerunner of New Atheism, is particularly vociferous in the science/faith dichotomy:

> *God and immorality, the central dogmas of the Christian religion, find no support in science...No doubt people will continue to entertain these beliefs because they are pleasant, just as it is pleasant to think ourselves virtuous and our enemies wicked...I do not pretend to be able to prove that there is no God. I equally cannot prove that Satan is a fiction. The Christian God may exist; so may the Gods of Olympus, or of ancient Egypt, or of Babylon.*[66]

Atheism points to, via the scientific endeavor, cultural progress that moves humanity away from faith positions and towards evidential understanding. Newton's mechanical astronomy replaced astrology, mathematical understandings of probability displaced luck, chemistry succeeded alchemy, city planning and social hygiene attenuate the effect of plagues, and medicine has moved toward germ theory.[67] As events like these pushed humanity into the age of science, superstition and magical thinking have been gradually reduced. However, New Atheism is reticent to admit the knowledge science has simultaneously opened up regarding the divine. Both at the macroscopic and microscopic levels, modern day cosmology and teleology suggest design which implies a designer. In the

---

[64] Shermer, *Believe*, 141.
[65] Baggini, *Introduction*, 32.
[66] Russell, *Christian*, 50.
[67] Shermer, *Believe*, 45.

words of physicist Freeman Dyson, "As we look out into the universe and identify the many accidents of physics and astronomy that have worked to our benefit, it almost seems as if the universe must in some sense have known that we were coming."[68]

Section 5 of 7
Moralism

Religious and Atheistic Points of Agreement

People who draw their worldview from historic Christianity generally believe that moral truth exists because God has woven it into the fabric of reality. Those without religious faith tend to think notions of good and evil are the products of evolutionary pressure and cultural invention.[69] It's noteworthy then to recognize that these two disparate groups, evangelical Christians and militant New Atheists, have strikingly similar views when it comes to *relativistic* morality, albeit identifying uniquely different origins.

Religious conservatives believe there are right answers to questions of meaning and morality; ordinary facts may certainly be discovered through rational inquiry, yet values ultimately have their inception with the divine. Secular liberal relativism, in contrast, tends to imagine that no objective answers to moral questions actually exist. Sam Harris bemoans, "Multiculturalism, moral relativism, political correctness, tolerance even of *intolerance* – these are the familiar consequences of separating facts and values on the left."[70] Harris's frustration with liberal relativism, and its inherent self-refuting nature, is obvious:

> To demand that the proud denizens of an ancient culture conform to our view of gender equality would be culturally imperialistic and philosophically naive. This is a surprisingly common view, especially among anthropologists. Moral relativism, however, tends to be self-contradictory. Relativists may say that moral truths exist only relative to a specific cultural framework – but this claim about the status of moral truth purports to be true across all possible frameworks.[71]

---

[68] Freeman Dyson, *Disturbing the Universe* (New York: Harper and Row, 1979), 250.
[69] Harris, *Landscape*, 2.
[70] Harris, *Landscape*, 5.

Congruent with Harris, cognitive scientist Steven Pinker shares a distaste for moral relativism as well. Pinker states with unveiled disgust:

> If only one person in the world held down a terrified, struggling screaming little girl, cut off her genitals with a septic blade, and sewed her back up, leaving only a tiny hole for urine and menstrual flow, the only question would be how severely that person should be punished...But when millions of people do this, instead of the enormity being magnified millions-fold, suddenly it becomes "culture"...and is even defended by some Western "moral thinkers," including feminists.[72]

Although Christians find in atheism an unexpected ally in their distinction from liberalism, the intellectual truce is minimal in scope. Harris, the most developed New Atheist thinker when it comes to moral theory, shares with his fellow atheists a vehemence toward divine-derived morality that is no less an intensity than his view of liberal relativism. Dennett, one of Harris's fellow "four horsemen," caustically considers the development of religious thought: "It was important to believe that somebody somewhere who knows what's right is telling you. Like Dumbo's magic feather, some crutches for the soul work only if you believe they do."[73]

Religious Morality Inferior to Atheistic Morality

Because historic Christianity conceives of morality first as a matter of obedience to God's revealed will, atheists mistakenly believe Scriptural precepts have nothing to do with maximizing well-being in this world.[74] Some atheists will argue that the teaching of Christ, as it appears in the Gospels, actually has little to do with a real-life, Christian ethic.[75] More so, most of the New Atheists will claim atheists are not only capable of leading moral lives, they are actually equipped for a superior morality when compared to religious believers who confuse divine law and punishment with right and wrong.[76]

Shermer's definition of religion is relevant in the context of a conversation on morality; he believes that religion developed as a social

---

[71] Harris, *Landscape*, 45.

[72] Steven Pinker, *The Blank Slate: The Modern Denial of Human Nature* (New York: Penguin, 2002), 273.

[73] Dennett, *Spell*, 134.

[74] Harris, *Landscape*, 63.

[75] Russell, *Christian*, 25.

[76] Baggini, *Introduction*, 37.

structure to enforce rules of human interaction before there were institutions such as the state. "Religion is a social institution that evolved as an integral mechanism of human culture to create and promote myths, to encourage altruism and reciprocal altruism, and to reveal the level of commitment to cooperate and reciprocate among members of the community."[77] This line of thinking is what informs the atheist's view that religious precepts date from a time when man was more cruel than he is in modern times, and therefore tended to perpetuate inhumanities which the moral conscience of the age would otherwise outgrow.[78]

Morality Determined Apart from Religion

Rather than rooting morality in *divine* decree, Harris believes a better grounding is found in the maximization of personal and collective well-being. Although everyone has an intuitive morality, Harris argues, much of that intuition is wrong and therefore society should foster moral experts who have a deep understanding of the causes and condition of human well-being.[79] It's not entirely clear if Harris views himself as one of these desired experts, but as an expert in neuroscience he is particularly interested in the neurological basis for human ethics. For instance, Harris points out that the scientific study of the brains of psychopaths or sociopaths has yielded considerable insight into the neural basis for morality. Neuroimaging of psychopaths when compared to non-psychopathic criminals and non-criminals exhibit significantly less activity in the regions of the brain that respond to emotional stimuli.

> *The medial prefrontal cortex (MPFC) is central to most discussions of morality and the brain... Injuries here have been associated with a variety of deficits including poor impulse control, emotional blunting, and the attenuation of social emotions like empathy, shame, embarrassment, and guilt. When frontal damage is limited to the MPFC, reasoning ability as well as the conceptual knowledge of moral norms are generally spared, but the ability to behave appropriately toward others tends to be disrupted.[80]*

If morality has no divine origin, then atheism is comfortable basing ethics on neurological underpinnings and human well-being. "Here is a first

---

[77] Shermer, *Believe*, 162.
[78] Russell, *Christian*, 30.
[79] Harris, *Landscape*, 36.
[80] Harris, *Landscape*, 93.

step in moral thinking. Forget any transcendental lawgiver or divine source of morality. Just think about what is needed for a human life to go well and...we have one pillar upon which to build a godless morality."[81] New Atheism claims that just as there exists no such thing as Christian physics or Muslim algebra, no need exists either for a religious-based ethic. Morality then, in the atheistic framework, can be considered an undeveloped branch of science, a branch where science should increasingly inform values.[82]

Atheistic Morality Must Borrow from Christian Morality

Perhaps the most challenging aspect of a godless morality is the awkward tendency New Atheism has to borrow from Christian morality in its moral definitions. At the outset, one is tempted to question Harris's perspective that maximizing human well-being is the best or most appropriate metric for morality. Why well-being? Why not instead choose to maximize compassion, education, or economic opportunity? Even if the tenuous "morality = well-being" definition is accepted though, the curious tendency to borrow from Christian ethics for moral definitions yet remains. "If we want to make a bet as insurance against the possibility of God's existence," Baggini states, "then we should be good, and the rest doesn't really matter."[83] The obvious question – "how is Baggini's "good" to be be defined? Whose well-being shall be the standard?"

Atheist historian Richard Carrier offers a textbook example for the self-refuting nature of godless morality:

> As a loving parent, I would think it a horrible failure on my part if I didn't educate my children well, and supervise them kindly, teaching them how to live safe and well, and warning them of unknown or unexpected dangers... It would be felony criminal neglect. Yet that is God: An absentee mom – who lets kids get kidnapped and murdered or run over by cars, who does nothing to teach them what they need to know, who never sits down like a loving parent to have an honest chat with them, and who would let them starve if someone else didn't intervene. As this is unconscionable, almost any idea of a god that fits the actual evidence of the world is unconscionable.[84]

---

[81] Baggini, *Introduction*, 49.
[82] Harris, *Landscape*, 4 & 21.
[83] Baggini, *Introduction*, 35.

Carrier desires to have it both ways. He declares morality a valid category apart from the divine, then holds God to the very moral code he declares God did not decree. A similar, though not atypical, error is made by Atheist author Ian McEwan.

The believers should know in their hearts by now that, even if they are right and there actually is a benign and watchful personal God, he is, as all the daily tragedies, all the dead children attest, a reluctant intervener. The rest of us, in the absence of any evidence to the contrary, know that it is highly improbable that there is anyone up there at all.[85]

McEwan's dissatisfaction with a God who permits tragedy once again begs the question: *upon who's objective standard is McEwan's moral indignation based?*

Atheist and radical animal rights activist Peter Singer identifies, perhaps most accurately, the consequences of Godless morality. If divine decree is taken off the table, then what right does humanity have to place any human well-being above that of any living creature – at the very least invertebrates. Singer can identify no such right.

Once we ask why it should be that all humans—including infants, mental defectives, psychopaths, Hitler, Stalin, and the rest—have some kind of dignity or worth that no elephant, pig, or chimpanzee can ever achieve, we see that this question is as difficult to answer as our original request for some relevant fact that justifies the inequality of humans and other animals.   When we consider members of our own species who lack the characteristics of normal human beings we can no longer say that their lives are always to be preferred to those of other animals... As long as we remember that we should give the same respect to the lives of animals as we give to the lives of those human beings at a similar mental level we shall not go far wrong.[86]

---

[84] Richard Carrier, *Sense and Goodness without God: A Defense of Metaphysical Naturalism* (Bloomington, IN: Author House, 2005), 281.

[85] Ian McEwan, "End of the World Blues," accessed on June 15, 2016, http://www.skeptic.ca /End_of_World_Blues.htm.

[86] Peter Singer, All Animals Are Equal, Accessed on July 15, 2016, http://spot.colorado.edu/~heathwoo /phil1200,Spr07/singer.pdf.

The Delusion of Religious Belief

One of the more intriguing aspects of New Atheist Christopher Hitchens's life is the connection between his intellectual ferocity (toward Christianity) and his moral beliefs. In his 2010 memoir, *Hitch 22*, Hitchens spends no small amount of time establishing his early exposure at boarding school to homo-eroticism and subsequent, homosexual relationships. "'He was a sort of strawberry blond, very slightly bow-legged, with a wicked smile that seemed to promise both innocence and experience. Were poems exchanged? Were there white-hot and snatched kisses? Did we sometimes pine for the holidays ... to be back at school? Yes, yes, and yes."[87] Hitchens's sexual proclivities are relevant to New Atheism's view of rationalism because they perfectly illustrate how attitude often informs view of intellect. "It was my first exposure to love as well as to sex, and it helped teach me as vividly as anything could have done that religion was cruel and stupid. One was indeed punishable for one's very nature: 'Created sick: commanded to be sound.'"[88]

Hitchens's admission that he views religion as "stupid" is symptomatic of the four horsemen of New Atheism, as well as most contemporary academics who fall beneath New Atheism's umbrella. Sam Harris is quick to draw parallels between religion and the *Diagnostic and Statistical Manual of Mental Disorders'* definition of delusion: a "false belief based on incorrect inference about external reality that is firmly sustained despite what almost everyone else believes and despite what constitutes incontrovertible and obvious proof or evidence to the contrary."[89]

Baggini states that "[w]ith religion, we are like children who still believe that we are protected in the world by benevolent parents who will look after us."[90] Richard Dawkins calls the Bible Belt "the reptilian brain of southern and middle America," in contrast to the "country's cerebral cortex to the north and down the coasts."[91] And Dennett states:

---

[87] Christopher Hitchens, *Hitch 22: A Memoir* (New York: Hatchette Book Group 2010), 76.

[88] Hitchen, *Memoir*, 76.

[89] Harris, *Landscape*, 58.

[90] Baggini, *Introduction*, 111.

[91] Naomi Schaefer Riley, "A Revelation: Civil Debate Over God's Existence," last accessed June 16, 2016, http://www.wsj.com/articles/SB119214767015956720.

The kindly God who lovingly fashioned each and every one of us (all creatures great and small) and sprinkled the sky with shining stars for our delight – that God is, like Santa Claus, a myth of childhood, not anything a sane, undeluded adult could literally believe in. That God must either be turned into a symbol for something less concrete or abandoned altogether.[92]

Atheism is eager to identify motivation on the part of religious folks for why they embrace antiquated ideas. Bertrand Russell does not imagine "the real reason why people accept religion has anything to do with argumentation. They accept religion on emotional grounds."[93] He adds, "Religion is based, I think, primarily and mainly upon fear... Fear is the parent of cruelty, and therefore it is no wonder if cruelty and religion have gone hand in hand."[94] Dennett agrees with the general assessment: "When you are faced with the often terrifying uncertainty of a dangerous world, the belief that *somebody is watching over you* may well be a decisively effective morale booster, capable of turning people who would otherwise be disabled by fear and indecision into stalwart agents."[95]

While it lies beyond the scope of this work to consider all variety of motivators unto religious faith, it is revealing – in light of the comments above – what Michael Shermer's research has uncovered.

It turns out that the number-one reason people give for why they believe in God is a variation on the classic cosmological or design argument: the good design, natural beauty, perfection, and complexity of the world or universe compels us to think that it could not have come about without an intelligent designer...Thus, contrary to what most religions preach about the need and importance of faith, most people believe because of reason.[96]

The Danger of Religious Belief

New Atheism is not content to deride religious conviction simply as delusion. Atheism further raises the concern that religious belief, in addition to its affront to reason, remains a clear and present *danger* to society. Atheist-turned-theist Antony Flew identifies the issue, "The chief

---

[92] Daniel Dennett, *Darwin's Dangerous Idea: Evolution and the Meanings of Life* (London: Simon & Schuster, 1996), 18.

[93] Russell, *Christian*, 19.

[94] Russell, *Christian*, 22.

[95] Dennett, *Spell*, 178.

[96] Shermer, *Believe*, xviii.

target of these [New Atheism] books is, without question, organized religion of any kind, time, or place." He goes on to identity the irony that these books themselves "read like fundamentalist sermons;" they are authored in effect by hellfire and brimstone preachers warning of dire retribution and even apocalypse if the religious do not turn from their ways.[97]

Flew's case is not overstated. Dennett seeks to establish the parallel between religion and what in legal parlance is referred to as an "attractive nuisance": things like unenclosed swimming pools, old refrigerators with their doors not removed, stacks of building materials or other dangerous items that can lure small children. "Those who maintain religions…must be held similarly responsible for the harms produced by some of those whom they attract… Until the priests and rabbis and imams and their flocks explicitly condemn *by name* the dangerous individuals and congregations within their ranks, they are *all* complicit."[98] Russell's condemnation of faith is clear, if nothing else, "My own view on religion is that of Lucretius. I regard it as a disease born of fear and as a source of untold misery to the human race."[99] He goes on:

> *Religion prevents our children from having a rational education; religion prevents us from removing the fundamental causes of war; religion prevents us from teaching the ethic of scientific co-operation in place of the old fierce doctrines of sin and punishment. It is possible that mankind is on the threshold of a golden age; but, if so, it will be necessary first to slay the dragon that guards the door, and this dragon is religion.[100]*

The Defense of Religious Belief

The fifteenth-century mathematician and physicist, Blaise Pascal, believed, "Men despise religion; they hate it, and fear it is true." It's unlikely many New Atheists would be comfortable going on record with agreement of Pascal's theory, for few are willing even to admit Christianity's rational underpinnings. Russell for instance maintains "it is amusing to hear the modern Christian telling you how mild and rationalistic Christianity really is… Gradual emasculation of the Christian doctrine has

---

[97] Flew, *Notorious*, xvi.
[98] Dennett, *Spell*, 299-301.
[99] Russell, *Christian*, 24.
[100] Russell, *Christian*, 47.

been effected in spite of the most vigorous resistance, and solely as the result of the onslaughts of freethinkers."[101]   But is Russell's statement true?   Sam Harris is forthright when he admits truth, in principle, has nothing to do with consensus. One person can be right and everyone else wrong. Consensus provides a snapshot view of what is happening in the world at a moment in time but in no way does general consensus constrain what may or may not be true.[102] This principle is a valuable one for Gospel-committed Christians in an age where militant atheism has dramatically increased the volume – and perhaps the commitment to – atheistic principles.

It is surprising how clear-headed Harris's take on truth is, given that he recognizes the rational implications of a godless existence. In his work *Free Will*, Harris argues strenuously for the absence of free will; he asserts that our thoughts come out of the darkness of prior causes which the conscious mind did not bring into being. "Free will is an illusion… thoughts and intentions emerge from background causes of which we are unaware and over which we exert no conscious control. We do not have the freedom we think we have."[103] This immediately raises the question, *if non-material consciousness is an illusion, and free will does not actually exist, what makes Harris's own thoughts valid?*

New Atheism will not accept the possibility that Bible-rooted Christianity has its grounding in an actual experience of the divine. Surprisingly, in its ever present search to identify the "real" (i.e. non-supernatural) motivation for faith, Dennett unwittingly begins moving toward the reality that religious thought often is intellectually measured. "Religious behavior – to the degree that it occurs – is generally based on cost-benefit calculations and is therefore rational behavior in precisely the same sense that other human behavior is rational."[104] For the committed Christian, this will be a back-handed compliment, but it does set the stage for a consideration of Christianity's inherently objective worldview. None other than Charles Darwin, for instance, in his 19th century autobiography, expressed a view of religion's reasonable conclusions:

---

[101] Russell, *Christian*, 36-37.
[102] Harris, *Landscape*, 31.
[103] Sam Harris, *Free Will* (New York: Free Press, A Division of Simon & Schuster, 2012), 5.
[104] Dennett, *Spell*, 183.

[Reason tells me of the] extreme difficulty or rather impossibility of conceiving this immense and wonderful universe, including man with his capability of looking far backwards and far into futurity, as the result of blind chance or necessity. When thus reflecting I feel compelled to look to a First Cause having an intelligent mind in some degree analogous to that of man; and I deserve to be called a theist.[105]

Antony Flew, who does not profess Christianity nor claim a religious experience of any sort, writes it was rational conclusions based on newly discovered scientific evidence that forced a rethinking of his previously held positions. "When I finally came to recognize the existence of God, it was not a paradigm shift, because my paradigm remains, as Plato in his *Republic* scripted his Socrates to insist: 'We must follow the argument wherever it leads'."[106] Flew's rational move toward theism was based on both the growing field of big bang cosmology as well as the newly discovered teleological complexity of DNA, Boyle's law, Newton's first law of motion, etc. "The important point is not merely that there are regularities in nature, but that these regularities are mathematically precise, universal, and "tied together"... The question we should ask is how nature came packaged in this fashion."[107] Similarly, Oxford professor and theist Richard Swinburne has little patience for elaborate theories without evidence that are used as work-arounds for atheism. "It is crazy to postulate a trillion (casually unconnected) universes to explain the features of one universe, when postulating one entity (God) will do the job."[108]

Section 7 of 7
Nihilism

Motives and the Search for Meaning

In his book *Waking Up*, Sam Harris moves from his *Free Will* question on the very existence of free will toward a perhaps even grander question: does a godless existence still allow for spirituality? Harris recognizes what

---

[105] Charles Darwin, *The Autobiography of Charles Darwin 1809-1882*, ed. Nora Barlow (London: Collins, 1958), 92-93.

[106] Flew, *Notorious*, 89.

[107] Flew, *Notorious*, 75 and 96.

[108] Richard Swimburne, "Design Defended," *Think* (Spring 2004), 17.

the Christian church has taught for centuries – the human condition is one that does little more than lurch between wanting and not wanting. Harris asks the obvious question: is there more to life than this?[109] He offers, "Our world is dangerously riven by religious doctrines that all educated people should condemn, and yet there is more to understanding the human condition than science and secular culture generally admit."[110]

The search for ultimate meaning, historically left to the religious and faith-based teachers, is one atheism is eager to take back. Baggini suggests the question of meaning is a vital one because if the only point in living is to serve somebody else's purpose, human beings cease to be valuable in their own right and become merely a tool for others. A creator God, according to Baggini, does not provide life with a meaning.[111] He continues:

> Religious people...see this world as a kind of preparation for the next. For these people, life isn't really valuable in itself at all. It is like a coin which can be exchanged for a good that really does count: the after-life. This merely postpones the question about what makes life worth living... It seems religion does not so much provide an answer as ask us to accept on trust that an answer will be forthcoming.[112]

It is unclear how much interaction Baggini has had with Bible-based Christianity, given that an "only-the-after-life-counts" view of existence is antithetical to both mainstream evangelicalism as well as Christ's direct teaching (see John 10:10). Regardless, it is clear that questions of purpose and motive run deep in the atheistic worldview.

As far back as Charles Darwin, there was recognition that any meaning in life is mitigated by the eventual demolition of consciousness. "Believing as I do that man in the distant future will be a far more perfect creature than he now is, it is an intolerable thought that he and all other sentient beings are doomed to complete annihilation... To those who fully admit the immortality of the human soul, the destruction of our world will not appear so dreadful."[113] Darwin's inference is that religion is motivated by the search for purpose. But atheist philosopher Aldous Huxley makes clear

---

[109] Sam Harris, *Waking Up: A Guide to Spirituality Without Religion* (New York: Simon & Schuster, 2014), 17.

[110] Harris, *Waking*, 6.

[111] Baggini, *Introduction*, 59.

[112] Baggini, *Introduction*, 66.

[113] Charles Darwin, *The Life and Letters of Charles Darwin* (New York: D. Appleton and Company, 1896), 282.

that the *absence* of meaning can be just as strong a motivator for worldview.

> *I had motives for not wanting the world to have a meaning, consequently assumed that it had none, and was able without any difficulty to find satisfying reasons for this assumption... The philosopher who finds no meaning in the world is not concerned exclusively with a problem in pure metaphysics; he is also concerned to prove that there is no valid reason why he personally should not do as he wants to do.*[114]

There is likely minimal value in attempting to decipher the *motives* for atheism's belief except to lay bare the potential hypocrisy of New Atheism's claim that it is only *religious* conviction that is motivated by worldly purpose. For instance, the suicide-pact death of Hitchens's mother with her adulterous lover, and subsequent coldness of the Anglican priest who presided over her funeral, clearly had a strong impact on Christopher Hitchens's view of religion.[115] Nihilist Friedrich Nietzche's early dose of syphilis caught during his first ever sexual encounter, together with its crushing migraine headaches, attacks of blindness, and metastasis into dementia and paralysis, certainly informed his view of ultimate deity and temporal meaning.[116] And none other than Bertrand Russell admits in his autobiography, "Nothing can penetrate the loneliness of the human heart except the highest intensity of the sort of love the religious teachers have preached."[117] Russell's daughter, a professing Christian, would later reflect on her father's fall from childhood faith, believing his "whole life was a search for God... Somewhere at the back of my father's mind, at the bottom of his heart, in the depths of his soul, there was an empty space that had once been filled by God, and he never found anything else to put in it."[118]

Despair at the Absence of Meaning

When one interacts with the scope of twentieth-century atheism and twenty-first century New Atheism, it is difficult to avoid the sense of crushing insignificance and nihilistic despair. Harris's search for godless

---

[114] Aldous Huxley, *Ends and Means* (London: Chatto & Windus, 1941), 270 and 272.
[115] Hitchen, *Hitch*, 26.
[116] Hitchens, *Mortality*, 60-61.
[117] Russell, *Autobiography*, 146.
[118] Flew, *Notorious*, xxi.

spirituality in *Waking Up* recognizes early on that, "Our pleasures, however refined or easily acquired, are by their very nature fleeting. They begin to subside the instant they arise, only to be replaced by fresh desires or feelings of discomfort."[119]   Physicist Lawrence Krauss places the fleeting nature of our existence in a cosmological context: "We continue to marshal the courage to live meaningful lives in a universe that likely came into existence, and may fade out of existence, without purpose, and certainly without us at its center."[120]

At the fiftieth anniversary of the United Nations in the Cathedral of St. John the Divine in New York City, the astronomer Carl Sagan waxed poetic about purpose and eternal significance. His comments tangentially echo the earlier discussion of religion as delusion and then move toward more universal implications:

> *One of science's alleged crimes is revealing that our favorite, most reassuring stories about our place in the universe and how we came to be are delusional... We have found from modern astronomy that we live on a tiny hunk of rock and metal third from the sun, that circles a humdrum star in the obscure outskirts of an ordinary galaxy, which contains some four hundred billion other stars, which is one of about a hundred billion other galaxies that make up the universe... In this perspective the idea that our planet is at the center of the universe, much less that human purpose is central to the existence of the universe, is pathetic.[121]*

If Sagan's comments offer an accurate rendering of the intellectual consequence of atheistic ideology, atheist and winner of the Nobel Prize for physics Steven Weinberg will do little to buoy the soul.

> *It is almost irresistible for humans to believe that we have some special relation to the universe, that human life is not just a more-or-less farcical outcome of a chain of accidents reaching back to the first three minutes, but that we were somehow built in from the beginning. It is even harder to realize that this present universe has evolved from an unspeakably unfamiliar early condition, and faces a future extinction of endless cold or intolerable heat. The more the universe seems comprehensible, the more it also seems pointless.[122]*

---

[119] Harris, *Waking*, 16-17.
[120] Krauss, *Nothing*, 148.
[121] Shermer, *Believe*, 214-215.
[122] Steven Weinberg, *The First Three Minutes* (United States: Basic Books, 1993), 154.

In June of 2010, Christopher Hitchens was diagnosed with esophageal cancer and his health began a steady descent until his eventual death in late 2011. Hitchens's book *Mortality*, published posthumously, provides a striking glimpse into the mind of the first widely-known New Atheist to face death. Hitchens writes of his cancer diagnosis:

> *I have been taunting the Reaper into taking a free scythe in my direction and have now succumbed to something so predictable and banal that it bores even me. Rage would be beside the point for the same reason. Instead, I am badly oppressed by the gnawing sense of waste...To the dumb question "Why me?" the cosmos barely bothers to return the reply: Why not?*[123]

Hitchens question of "why" is one the Christian faith seeks to tackle boldly and head on. The purpose of life, humanity's inherent dignity – these categories are not separate from Scripture's view of cosmological origin or God-derived morality. When a Godless reality is propagated however, New Atheism is left with no grounding in which to rest questions of meaning and significance. Krauss is honest about the implications:

> *Based on everything we know about the universe is the possibility that the future, perhaps the infinite future, is one in which nothingness will once again reign. If we live in a universe whose energy is dominated by the energy of nothing, as I have described, the future is indeed bleak. The heavens will become cold and dark and empty. But the situation is actually worse. A universe dominated by the energy of empty space is the worst of all universes for the future of life. Any civilization is guaranteed to ultimately disappear in such a universe, starved of energy to survive... In this case, the answer to the question, "Why is there something rather than nothing?" will then simply be: "There won't be for long."*[124]

---

[123] Hitchens, *Mortality*, 5-6.
[124] Krauss, *Nothing*, 180.

Introduction

The "unexamined life" Socrates once spoke of, one he deemed "not worth living," bears striking resemblance to the life many seem to have slipped into within the the Western world. In the prosperous, first-world, American context, many are diverted, but not conscious of it. This life of constant distraction becomes a seedbed for spiritual apathy and doctrinal antipathy. Os Guinness observes, "Focused attention has become the rarest commodity in the world. Everyone is speaking, no one is listening, and the resulting familiarity breeds inattention. It is...difficult to break through the many levels of resistance and make fresh sense to people."[1]

The Project Design presented in this chapter has been an attempt to "make fresh sense" to the local church by examining and responding to the primary tenets and presuppositions of New Atheism. It is the researcher's conviction that authentic dialogue with unbelief is vital if American Christianity's next generation is to recover from the church's increasingly flaccid and non-influential position in culture. In a recent sociological study, teens were asked why they had fallen away from the religion in which they were raised. Researchers presupposed they would primarily hear of emotional or relationship issues. To the researcher's surprise

---

[1] Guinness, OS, *Fool's Talk: Recovering The Art of Christian Persuasion* (Downers Grove, IL: InterVarsity Press, 2015), 180.

however, the most frequent answer given by the project participants for leaving the church was their unanswered doubts and questions.[2] Similarly, a Barna study revealed 36 percent of young adults felt they could not ask "life's most pressing questions in church" even as 23 percent of those surveyed had "significant intellectual doubts" about Christian teaching.[3] Peter Hitchens, professed Christian and brother to New Atheist Christopher Hitchens, ominously observed in 2010:

> When I am in church in England now, I notice that it is people of around my age (I was born in 1951) who are mostly absent. There are plenty who are older than seventy or younger than forty, but very few in between. In the United States, I suspect that a great defection of the same kind is now under way in the college generation and that those now in college, or having recently left it, are most hostile − or perhaps worse, indifferent − to religion than any previous American generation. One orthodoxy is giving way to another, as happened in Britain.[4]

Section 1 of 2
Project Design

The design of this research project involved three steps which, taken together, formed a classic pretest/posttest quasi-experiment. Subjects were studied, via volunteer survey participation, both before and after experimental manipulation. The primary purpose of the project was to measure and potentially adjust American views − primarily but not exclusively those of evangelical Christians in New England − regarding several categories related to atheism. The pretest and posttest surveys were sandwiched around a six-week sermon series delivered to a mid-sized New England church.

---

[2] Christian Smith and Melinda Lundquist Denton, *Soul Searching: The Religious and Spiritual Lives of American Teenagers* (Oxford: Oxford University Press, 2005), 89.

[3] David Kinnaman, *You Lost Me: Why Young Christians Are Leaving Church and Rethinking Faith* (Grand Rapids, MI: Baker Books, 2011), 190.

[4] Peter Hitchens, *The Rage Against God: How Atheism Led Me to Faith* (Grand Rapids, MI: Zondervan, 2010), 9-10.

Pretest Survey

The twenty-four question pretest was designed using a paid membership on SurveyMonkey.com and made available to volunteer participants exclusively online. The survey opportunity was announced verbally at Medway Community Church's (MCC) Sunday gatherings and electronically through MCC's weekly email newsletter, as well as through the researcher's Facebook account. The pretest survey went live on March 9, 2016 and was closed approximately 3 weeks later on March 31, prior to the start of the sermon series.

The survey, which can be found in its entirety in Appendix A, was broken into four sections on five electronic pages. Page 1 welcomed the participant, thanked them for their involvement, and briefly explained the survey's use in the researcher's doctoral studies. This welcome page also explained the four-section structure of the survey, identified an expected completion time of 5-6 minutes, and stressed that the survey was completely anonymous.

Section 1 of the pretest survey was composed of seven demographic questions. These questions included gender, age, ethnicity, and region of residence. The demographic questions also inquired about educational background, religious affiliation, and current career field.

Section 2 of the pretest survey was labeled "Social Engagement with Atheism." This section, composed of seven questions, sought to identify the subject's social interaction, if any, with those who possessed atheistic convictions. It also measured the participant's perception of atheism's presence in the culture regionally, nationally, and worldwide.

Section 3 of the pretest survey was labeled "Personal Engagement with Atheism." This section, composed of four questions, sought to identity the subject's personal knowledge of atheistic dogma in areas like general worldview, morality, origin of the universe, and life purpose. Section 3 also measured the subject's confidence in the Bible to respond to atheism as well as the subject's personal inclination toward atheism despite public, religious affiliation.

The 4th and final section of the survey was labeled "Optional Responses." Unlike the previous sections, the four questions in this section allowed for open-ended responses. These questions inquired about the participant's desire to be better equipped for spiritual conversation with an atheist, areas the participant found atheism to be most and least convicting, and any other miscellaneous comments or ideas.

Over the course of its open period, the pretest survey was submitted by 333 respondents. All age demographics were represented except those under the age of 18. All regions of the country were represented except the South West. All religious affiliations were represented except Muslim. All ethnicities, career fields, and educational backgrounds were represented without exception. The overwhelming number of responses in the pretest came from white, Christian-affiliated individuals in New England.

Sermon Series

The six-part sermon series, which can be found in its entirety in Appendix B, was designed to respectfully and honestly present the worldview of contemporary atheists. This presentation invited the listener to question if the atheistic worldview is the best and most coherent representation of reality or if the Scriptures provide something more intellectually satisfying.[5] Throughout the sermon series, particular emphasis was placed on the self-labeled "four horsemen" of New Atheism (Richard Dawkins, Christopher Hitchens, Sam Harris, and Daniel Dennett).

The six-part sermon series, titled "The God Who is There: A Study on Belief and Unbelief," began on April 3rd and was preached over the course of seven consecutive Sundays, with a one Sunday break between sermons 2 and 3. The final sermon in the series was preached on May 15th. Based upon the Romans 1 examination presented in chapter 2 of this paper, the series' overall emphasis was that "every time you suppress a truth, an untruth takes its place." The researcher sought to posit that atheism, at its root, is formed by a series of truth suppressions surrounding various topics and categories. Once these suppressions are identified, the listener is encouraged to substitute these truth suppressions with Biblical precept. The primary topics of the individual sermons were as follows:

1. **Week 1:** An Introduction to Atheism and a homiletical presentation of Romans 1:18.
2. **Week 2:** Philosophical Materialism and a homiletical presentation of Romans 1:19-20.
3. **Week 3:** Scientism and a homiletical presentation of Romans 1:21.

---

[5] Audio recordings of these sermons, including their accompanying PowerPoint presentations, can be found at http://www.nowsprouting.com/medwaycommunitychurch/media.php?pageID=37.

4. **Week 4:** Moralism and a homiletical presentation of Romans 1:22.
5. **Week 5:** Nihilism and a homiletical presentation of Romans 1:23.
6. **Week 6:** Idolatry and a homiletical presentation of Romans 1:24-25.

Over the course of the sermon series, but particularly in weeks 4-6, the researcher sought to further introduce the concept of "functional atheism." This was defined as the Christian's tendency to profess Biblical belief yet *functionally* live as if God is non-existent, or at least personally uninvolved, in the individual's life.

The sermons were delivered in a church that averages slightly above 400 individuals for weekend attendance across two Sunday services. MCC is a 266 year old congregation; it meets in a traditional New England church building but uses a contemporary style of worship while retaining a few traditional elements. The congregation is multi-generational in makeup, casual in style of dress, and mostly middle to upper middle class in socio-economic status. The average sermon length in the series was 31 minutes.

Posttest Survey

The twenty-seven question posttest was announced verbally at one of Medway Community Church's (MCC) Sunday gatherings and electronically through MCC's email newsletter. Unlike the pretest, the posttest was not advertised on Facebook because completion of the posttest survey was only desired from those who had listened to some portion of the sermon series. The posttest survey went live on May 18, 2016, three days after the sermon series was concluded. The survey closed approximately 3 weeks later on June 4.

The survey, which can be found in its entirety in Appendix C, was separated into four sections on five electronic pages and closely mirrored the pretest survey. The only differences between the pretest and the posttest were:

- Section 1, Demographic Information, added a question to determine the number of sermons (0 to 6) the participant had heard from the recent sermon series.
- Section 3, Personal Engagement with Atheism, added a question about the participant's understanding of atheistic views surrounding science. Section 3 also added two questions

inquiring if the sermon series increased the participant's confidence in Christianity, and whether the sermon series left the participant better equipped to defend their Christian faith.

- Section 4, the optional open-ended questions, were altered from the pretest to now inquire about the participant's view of the recent sermon series: how was it helpful (if at all) and how could it have been improved?

Over the course of its open period, the posttest survey was completed by 135 respondents. All age demographics were represented except those under the age of 18. All regions of the country were represented except the Mid-West and Pacific States. The only religious affiliations represented were Christian and atheist and other (self-described as "believer"). All ethnicities were represented except Asian. All career fields were represented and all educational backgrounds were represented except those who had not yet acquired a High School degree or equivalent . Similar to the pretest, the overwhelming number of responses in the posttest came from white, Christian-affiliated individuals in New England.

Section 2 of 2
General Observations

Following the survey close dates, Christopher Gooley, founder and president of ETS Marketing Science, volunteered his services for statistical analysis and data review.[6] ETS has expertise in a broad array of statistical, econometric, and data mining techniques and was able to provide a professional analysis of both the pretest and posttest survey's constructions, as well as a determination of statistical significance throughout the results. Although in-depth survey results will be explored in chapter 5, this section will offer a brief review of the survey's factor analysis as well as general observations from the metadata.

---

[6] http://etsmarketingscience.com ETS has worked with numerous market leaders in industries including media and entertainment, pharmaceuticals, automotive, financial services, consumer packaged goods, retail, entertainment, and technology. For the past several years, Gooley has had a close working relationship with several executives at Disney.

To better understand the way in which the pretest survey was interpreted by the participants, a statistical technique known as a principal components analysis was conducted. This correlation analysis, married to a factor analysis with vary max rotation, determined which of the pretest survey's central questions (not including demographic and open-ended questions) were most strongly correlated in the minds of the respondents. Results of this analysis identified four primary categories which can be labeled as follows:

1. **Personal Engagement with Atheists:** Questions #8 and #9 on the pretest survey.
2. **Perceived Growth in Atheism:** Questions #11, #12, #13, and #14, on the pretest.
3. **Personal Understanding of Atheism:** Questions #10, #15, #16, #17, #18 on the pretest.
4. **Christianity vs Atheism:** unlike the previous three categories, this final category displayed a strong negative correlation between two questions. The negative correlation was not unexpected, as the two questions #19 and #20 measured first the respondents view of the Bible's convincing response to atheism followed by the respondent's personal predilection for atheism.

A review of both the pretest and posttest surveys has identified several noteworthy results to be further explored in chapter 5. A few summary statements regarding the factor analysis categories are as follows:

1. **Personal Engagement with Atheism:** Although there was a minor increase in results between the pretest and posttest surveys, these results offered no statistically significant change.
2. **Perceived Growth in Atheism:** Posttest surveys, when compared to the pretest, indicated no significant increase in the perceived growth of atheism either regionally or nationally. However, there was a statistical increase in the perceived growth of atheism *worldwide*.
3. **Personal Understanding of Atheism:** Across all five questions in this section, following the sermon series there were statistically significant improvements in the respondent's perceived understanding.
4. **Christianity vs Atheism:** Following the sermon series, there was a statistically significant increase in respondent's

conviction that the Bible offers a convincing response to an atheistic understanding of reality. Likewise, there was a statistically significant decrease in respondent's inclination toward atheism as their personal conviction.

Although additional information, in-depth results, and the researcher's own critique of the project design, will be examined in the following chapter, a high level review of the project suggests, with expert analysis confirming the results, two overarching conclusions:

1. The pretest/posttest quasi-experiment was appropriately constructed to allow for the measurement of statistically significant results.

The overall results of the six-part sermon series on engaging with atheism did result in a measureable *increase* in perceived understanding of the atheistic worldview, a measurable *increase* in respondents' Biblical confidence, and a measureable *decrease* in personal inclination toward atheism.

CHAPTER FIVE
Project Outcomes: Analysis and Interpretation

Introduction

Beyond the high level review of survey results touched upon in chapter 4, this chapter will more specifically consider each of the individual questions within the pretest and posttest surveys. In concert with the the statistical analysis and data review provided by ETS Marketing Science[1], interpretation of the data will be offered after a brief description of the survey question and respondent results. When appropriate, additional speculation may be suggested to account for either expected or unexpected results.

---

[1] Christopher Gooley, founder and president of ETS Marketing Science, http://etsmarketingscience.com.

FIGURE 1: Gender Demographics, pretest vs posttest

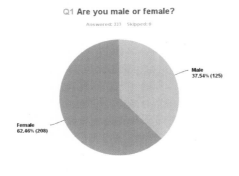

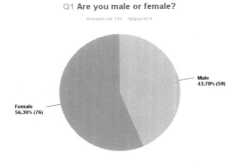

In each of the two surveys, responses by gender skewed female. The pretest returned 62% female and 38% male, while the posttest was slightly more balanced returning 56% female and 44% male. The gender-participation difference between the surveys may be explained by the dissemination of the pretest but not posttest via Facebook, which has a significantly higher population of women than men engaged on the social network.[2]

---

[2] Maeve Duggan, *The Demographics of Social Media Users*, last accessed on June 28, 2016, http://www.pewinternet.org/2015/08/19/the-demographics-of-social-media-users/. According to the 2015 Pew Research study referenced in this article, 77% of Americans using Facebook are female.

FIGURE 2: Age Demographics, pretest vs posttest

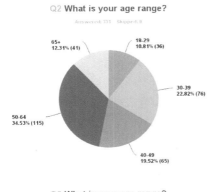

Q2 What is your age range?

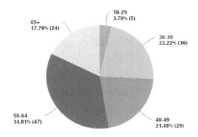

Both surveys returned similar results in age demographics; the 50-64 bracket returned over 1/3 of the total results followed by the 30-39 bracket which returned over 1/5 of the results. The exception to consistency between surveys occurred within the 18-29 year age bracket, which saw a drop-off from 11% of respondents in the pretest to just 4% of respondents in the posttest. This change may be explained by a smaller population of 18-29 year olds at Medway Community Church than those represented on Facebook. However, this drop off in 18-29 year old responses (36 individuals to just 5 individuals) was sharper than preferred.

FIGURE 3: Race Demographics, pretest vs posttest

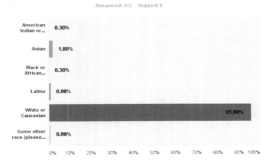

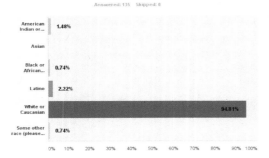

In each of the surveys, white or Caucasian ethnicities were the overwhelming representation at 95% of respondents. All other ethnicities had at least marginal representation in the pretest, while posttest results returned no Asian responses. The results were in line with expectations, given that Medway Community Church's demographics as well as the researcher's Facebook contacts are majority Caucasian.

FIGURE 4: Region of Residence, pretest vs posttest

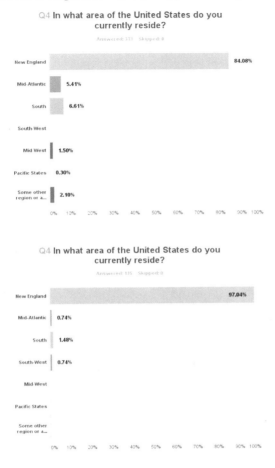

Area of residence questions on each of the surveys returned no unexpected results. The pretest survey, which included Facebook dissemination, collected results from all American regions except the South-West with the most number of results coming from New England (84%). The second and third highest regions represented were the South (7%) and the Mid-Atlantic (5%); prior to residence in New England, the researcher previously lived in each of these regions and therefore possessed the highest number of Facebook contacts from these areas.

The posttest survey was completed almost entirely by those who identified New England as their region of residence (97%). These results are intuitive given the sermon series was only delivered in New England. The few posttest surveys completed by those living outside New England were likely submitted by individuals listening to the sermon series online.

FIGURE 5: Education demographics, pretest vs posttest

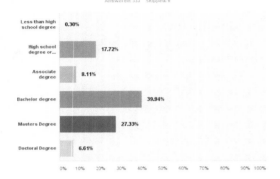

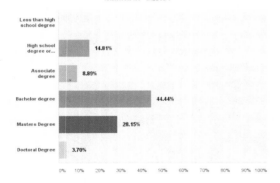

Across the two surveys, there was consistency regarding educational background. Completion of a bachelor's degree was the most common educational profile in both the pretest and posttest (40% and 44%, respectively). This was followed by completion of a Master's degree (27% and 28%) then High School degree (18% and 15%). In each of the surveys, there was a small number of responses from those who had completed a doctoral degree (7% and 4%) and in the pretest only, there was a single response collected from an individual who had completed less than a high school degree.

FIGURE 6: Religious Affiliation, pretest vs posttest

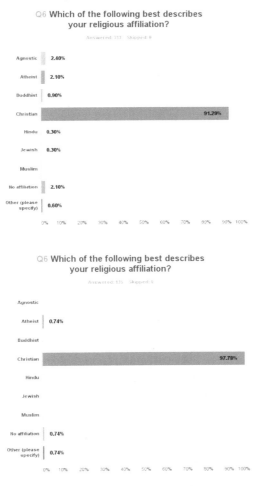

As expected, the Facebook disseminated pretest gathered results that were more varied in the category of religious affiliation than the MCC only posttest. The pretest returned at least some representation from all religious affiliations except Muslim, although Christian was the predominant response (91%). The posttest was dominated by those self-labeling as Christian (98%); atheist, no affiliation, and other were represented at less than 1% each.

In the pretest, results were filtered for the 18-29 age bracket (a total of 36 individuals); filtering reveals the percentage of self-labeled Christians in this 18-29 bracket decreased significantly from the overall percentage of 91% to 78%. Correspondingly, a marked increase for this bracket occurred for agnostic (2% to 8%) and atheist (2% to 6%).

FIGURE 7: Employment, pretest vs posttest

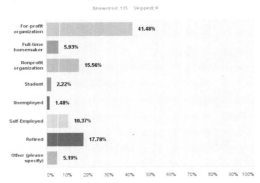

Across both the pretest and posttest surveys, respondents most frequently categorized their current job as a for-profit organization (42% and 41%). In the pretest survey, the category of "other" was selected 20% of the time, with the responses filled in most frequently as either "retired" or "self-employed." As a result, these two categories were added to the posttest survey, where retired (18%) and nonprofit organization (16%) were the second and third most frequently indicated employment condition.

FIGURE 8: Sermons Heard, posttest only

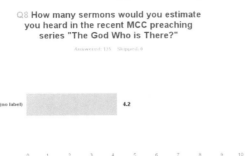

Q8 How many sermons would you estimate you heard in the recent MCC preaching series "The God Who is There?"

Answered: 135   Skipped: 6

(no label)   4.2

0   1   2   3   4   5   6   7   8   9   10

The final question within the demographics section of the surveys, regarding total sermons heard, was made available on the posttest survey only. For the 135 respondents, the average number of sermons heard in the six-part series was 4.2 sermons. This average dropped precipitously for the 18-29 age demographic (only 1.8 sermons heard on average) and increased slightly for the 50-64 age bracket (4.6 sermons heard). A single individual who self-labeled as atheist on the posttest listened to 5 of the 6 sermons.

Section 2 of 4
Social Engagement with Atheism

Section 2 of the pretest and posttest surveys was designed to measure the respondent's social engagement with atheism. Questions assessed both the participant's social interaction with atheists as well as their perception of atheist's overall presence in the culture. Each question invited the participant to respond with a selection of 1 through 5, which scaled from strongly disagree (1) → tend to disagree (2) → neutral (3) → tend to agree (4) → strongly agree (5). "I don't know" was also made available as a non-weighted selection.

FIGURE 9: Day-to-day Conversation with Atheists, pretest vs posttest

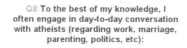

When asked if the respondent often had day-to-day conversation with atheists about casual topics, the results (3.47) were precisely identical between the posttest and pretest. This would suggest the sermon series did not have an immediate effect on the listener's proactive seeking out and social engagement of those with atheistic convictions. On the pretest, the score for this question was significantly higher for the 36 respondents who fell within the 18-29 age bracket (3.91). As one might expect given workplace diversity, scores were also higher on both surveys for those who work in a for-profit organization.

FIGURE 10: Spiritual Conversation with Atheists, pretest vs posttest

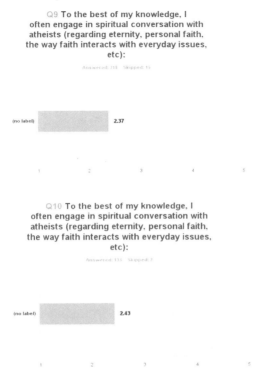

When asked about the frequency of spiritual conversation with atheists, there was no significant difference between the pretest and the posttest results.

FIGURE 11: Equipped to Defend Religious Faith, pretest vs posttest

Q10 I feel well equipped to explain and defend my religious faith in conversation with an atheist:

Answered: 318 Skipped: 15

Q11 I feel well equipped to explain and defend my religious faith in conversation with an atheist:

Answered: 133 Skipped: 2

When asked to evaluate how well equipped they are to defend their religious faith in conversation with an atheist, there was a statistically significant lift between the pretest (3.61) and posttest (3.88). This increase suggests the series was effective at equipping individuals for an apologetic endeavor; the increase was most noticeable among those who had heard all six sermons, given their score increased to 4.08.

In both the pretest and posttest, a noteworthy gap existed between scores for each gender. Women ranked statistically lower than men on both the pretest (3.53 female vs 3.92 male) and posttest (3.67 female vs 4.16 male). This poses an intriguing question for further study: why do men have a higher confidence in their ability to defend the Christian faith? In addition, on the pretest, the 288 individuals from New England scored themselves considerably less equipped (3.69) to defend their Christian faith than the 22 individuals from the South (4.29). This discrepancy could be related to a higher population of atheists in the Northeast.

FIGURE 12: Atheism's Regional Increase, pretest vs posttest

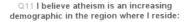

Q11 I believe atheism is an increasing
demographic in the region where I reside:

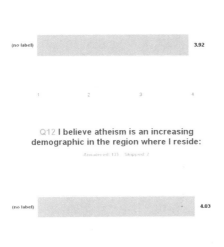

Q12 I believe atheism is an increasing
demographic in the region where I reside:

Between the two surveys, no significant change was observed in views on atheism's increase in the respondent's region.   On the pretest, not surprisingly, those living in New England were more likely to perceive an increase an atheism (4.05) while those in the South and Mid-Atlantic (3.43) were less likely to see an increase.   In addition, when filtered for educational background, those with a master's degree (3.75) or doctoral degree (3.9) were least likely to perceive a regional increase of atheism. This result may be related to a higher population of atheism among those with advanced degrees; in other words, familiarity with atheism had already been present for those with advanced academics. When moving to the posttest, those in the oldest age bracket of 65+ were least likely (3.62) to perceive an increase of atheism in their region.

FIGURE 13: Atheism's National Increase, pretest vs posttest

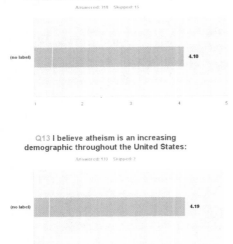

Q12 I believe atheism is an increasing
demographic throughout the United States:

Answered: 318   Skipped: 15

(no label) 4.10

Q13 I believe atheism is an increasing
demographic throughout the United States:

Answered: 133   Skipped: 2

(no label) 4.19

Although overall scores were higher than the previous "regional" question, pretest and posttest scores (4.1 and 4.19, respectively) remained similar when the respondent was asked about the perceived *national* increase of atheism in the United States.   Those from the Mid-Atlantic states (3.72) were least likely among regions to perceive a national increase in atheism.   When filtered for education, those who had acquired no greater than a High School or equivalent degree were least likely to perceive a national increase in atheism (3.78).

124

FIGURE 14: Atheism's Global Increase, pretest vs posttest

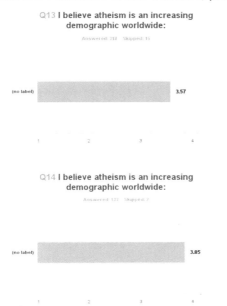

Q13 I believe atheism is an increasing
demographic worldwide:

Answered: 318   Skipped: 15

(no label)   3.57

1   2   3   4   5

Q14 I believe atheism is an increasing
demographic worldwide:

Answered: 133   Skipped: 2

(no label)   3.85

1   2   3   4   5

Among the three "perceived increase" questions, the question regarding atheism's *global* increase was the only one to return a statistically significant lift from pretest (3.57) to posttest (3.85). The pretest results showed that, when filtering for age, those 65+ were most likely to perceive a global increase in atheism (4.1). This was a curious result that seems contrary to previous data; when asked about *regional* increase, this same 65+ bracket returned low scores, suggesting a minimal increase of atheism in their context.

FIGURE 15: Atheism Outspokenness, pretest vs posttest

A statistically significant increase was displayed between pretest and posttest (4.12 vs 4.29) regarding the perceived outspokenness of present day atheists when compared to twenty years prior. When filtered for education, the pretest returned the lowest results among those who had no greater than High School degree or equivalent (4.07). However, in a surprising turn, it was those on the opposite end of the educational spectrum, those with a doctoral degree, who returned the lowest score on the posttest (3.75). It would seem that following the sermon series, those with the highest academic achievement – perhaps because they have been surrounded by atheists for some time – perceive no significant change in the volume of present-day atheism.

Section 3 of 4
Personal Engagement with Atheism

Section 3 of the surveys was designed to measure the respondent's own engagement with atheistic doctrine. Questions assessed the participant's understanding of the atheistic worldview, their belief in the viability of Scripture to answer atheistic doctrine, and their personal predilection for atheistic convictions. Like the previous section, each question invited the participant to respond with a selection of 1 through 5, which scaled from strongly disagree (1) → tend to disagree (2) → neutral (3) → tend to agree (4) → strongly agree (5). "I don't know" was also made available as a non-weighted selection.

FIGURE 16: Understanding Atheistic Worldview, pretest vs posttest

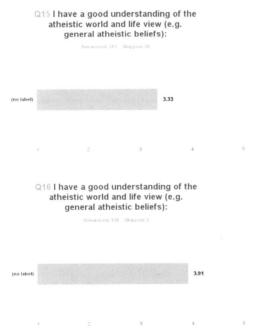

Among the four "understanding" questions considered on both the pretest and posttest, all four showed a statistically significant lift *following* the sermon series. All four questions also returned significantly higher scores for men than women. The first of these "understanding" questions, which inquired of the respondent's comprehension regarding the atheistic worldview, saw a score increase from 3.33 to 3.91. As one might expect, the lowest posttest scores were returned by those who only heard 0 to 3 sermons, as opposed to those who listened to between 4 and 6 sermons.

FIGURE 17: Understanding Atheistic Morality, pretest vs posttest

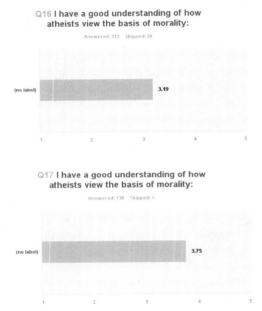

Q16 I have a good understanding of how atheists view the basis of morality:

Answered: 313   Skipped: 20

Q17 I have a good understanding of how atheists view the basis of morality:

Answered: 138   Skipped: 5

Overall understanding of atheistic morality increased between the pretest (3.19) and posttest (3.75). The lowest posttest scores belonged to the eleven individuals who heard zero sermons (3.11) while the highest scores belonged to those who heard all six sermons (4.08). On the pretest, the 280 individuals living in New England indicated the lowest understanding of atheistic morality (3.27) while the 22 individuals living in the south indicated the highest understanding (3.76).

FIGURE 18: Understanding Atheistic View of Origins, pretest vs posttest

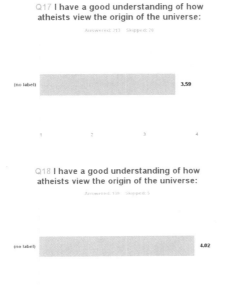

Survey participants were asked to rate their understanding of how atheists view the origin of the universe. There was a statistically significant increase from before the sermon series (3.59) to after (4.02), and both surveys showed, when filtering for career, the highest scores were among those who work in a for-profit organization. However, the lowest career scores changed from full-time homemakers in the pretest (3.32) to those who work in a non-profit organization on the posttest (3.71).

FIGURE 19: Understanding Atheistic View of Purpose, pretest vs posttest

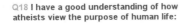

Q18 I have a good understanding of how
atheists view the purpose of human life:

Answered: 313   Skipped: 20

Q19 I have a good understanding of how
atheists view the purpose of human life:

Answered: 130   Skipped: 5

Among all questions on the survey, the greatest lift in overall score was seen in the respondent's perceived understanding of how atheists view the purpose of human life (moving from 3.16 to 3.72). Like the other "understanding" questions on the pretest, men (3.55) rated themselves significantly higher than women (3.07), and when filtered for education, those with a doctoral degree rated their understanding highest (3.62). In something of a surprise, rather than the expected 0 to 2 sermons, the lowest posttest score for this question was returned by the forty individuals who heard 3 or 4 sermons (3.45) while the highest score belonged to the seventy-three individuals who heard 5 or 6 sermons (3.9).

FIGURE 20: The Biblical Response to Atheism, pretest vs posttest

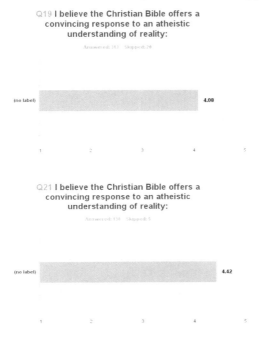

Q19 I believe the Christian Bible offers a convincing response to an atheistic understanding of reality:

Answered: 313 Skipped: 20

(no label) 4.08

Q21 I believe the Christian Bible offers a convincing response to an atheistic understanding of reality:

Answered: 138 Skipped: 5

(no label) 4.42

Confidence in the Bible's ability to refute atheism increased following the sermon series (from 4.08 to 4.42); while affirming to the preacher, this was likely due in part to a lower percentage of non-Christians in the posttest sample. On the pretest, when factored for age, the lowest score for this question was returned by those 18-29 (3.52), while the highest confidence in the Bible was indicated by those 65+ (4.59). Following the sermon series, however, the 18-29 age bracket saw a significant increase in score (to 4.2); the 65+ bracket (4.77) remained on the posttest the group most confident the Bible offers a convincing response to atheism.

FIGURE 21: Personal Inclination Toward Atheism, pretest vs posttest

Q20 Regardless of my publicly stated religion, I increasingly lean toward atheism as my own personal conviction:

Answered: 313   Skipped: 28

Q24 Regardless of my publicly stated religion, I increasingly lean toward atheism as my own personal conviction:

Answered: 130   Skipped: 5

The survey question the researcher was most curious to see returned was the one referenced in figure 21, regarding the respondent's personal conviction toward atheism regardless of public, religious affiliation. There was a slight, statistically insignificant decrease between the pretest and posttest, while scores for male vs female remained quite similar or identical across both surveys. The most noteworthy data for this question, when filtering for age, inverted the previous "confidence in the Bible" question. On both the pretest and posttest, those age 18-29 agreed the most with a personal leaning toward atheism, although inclination toward atheism did decrease following the sermon series (from 2.03 to 1.6). When filtered for sermons heard, those who indicated on the posttest the strongest inclination toward atheism were also those who only heard 0 to 2 sermons.

FIGURE 22: Understanding Atheistic View of Science, posttest only

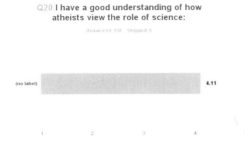

Q20 I have a good understanding of how
atheists view the role of science:

Answered: 138   Skipped: 5

(no label)   4.11

  1   2   3   4   5

In addition to the "both-survey" questions reviewed above, three more questions were added for the posttest only. The first of these questions, which measured perceived understanding of atheistic views of science, displayed a significantly higher score for men (4.27) than women (3.99). Consistent with expectations, those with masters (4.35) and doctoral degrees (4.8) also indicated a high level of understanding atheistic views of science.

FIGURE 23: Sermon Series More Confident and Better Equipped, posttest only

Q22 The recent MCC preaching series "The God Who is There" has left me MORE confident of the Christian faith than I was before?

Answered: 130   Skipped: 5

(no label)   3.98

Q23 The recent MCC preaching series "The God Who is There" has left me BETTER equipped to defend the Christian faith than I was before?

Answered: 130   Skipped: 5

(no label)   3.98

When asked if the preaching series left the the respondent more confident of the Christian faith and when asked if the preaching series left the respondent better equipped to defend the Christian faith, 130 respondents replied with an identical, average score for each of "tend to agree" (3.98). For each question, when filtered for age, those in the 18-29 bracket were least likely to have been helped by the sermon series, while those in the 30-39 age bracket were most likely to indicate the sermon series was helpful. These results are likely due to two factors. First, the 18-29 age bracket on average listened to only 1.8 sermons total. Second, Medway Community Church has a high population of new converts in the 30-39 age range, and therefore these individuals likely perceived the greatest gain from the teaching series.

The fourth and final section of the pretest and posttest surveys contained a few open-ended questions designed to allow the respondent to raise additional ideas not tested for in the preceding sections. Although not statistically helpful like the scored sections, open-ended questions did allow for personalized feedback to the researcher. Primary themes from the responses are considered below for each question. Several of the themes from the pretest questions were used to shape the sermon series that followed.

Pretest Open-Ended Question #1: In what way(s), if any, would you like to be better equipped to defend your religious faith while in conversation with an atheist?

Of 182 responses offered to this question, most fell into one of four broad categories. The first category was an expressed desire to be bolder and more courageous in conversation with non-Christians, the second was a desire to be more knowledgeable of atheistic tenets, and a third was the desire to be more familiar with Christian Scripture.

A large number of responses, composing the fourth category, centered on the participant's desire to be prepared with a "system" of Christian apologetics. Typical responses spoke of "5-10 biblical points as a starting point to defend faith," advance preparation of a "two-minute 'elevator speech'" and "practice role playing with a well-versed Christian in a class." These responses are intriguing given that in recent years, the contemporary emphasis in evangelical circles has been less focused on systems of evangelism, instead stressing the importance of dialogue and relationship. One area of potential, future research would be to investigate how preferences and perceived usefulness for programmatic approaches break out along age demographics.

The fourth and final category of responses to this question expressed a desire to more effectively show grace to non-Christians. "I think many atheists," suggested one participant, "become defensive and antagonistic when discussing religion because they feel their beliefs are not respected by most folks and they feel like they are being attacked." A separate response stated, "Relationships are more important than talking points," and another respondent offered, "I think the idea of grace to an atheist confuses them. I'd like to hone in on that better and be able to explain the story of the Bible and context of a relationship with God, with grace as the crux of the argument."

Pretest Open-Ended Question #2: Which atheistic belief(s), if any, do you find least convincing?

When asked which atheistic beliefs the respondent found *unconvincing*, most of the 171 responses broke down into three categories. The first category, capturing the majority of responses, had to do with creationism vs the credulity of non-theistic, universal origins. Respondents expressed doubt that "the universe just came into being on its own (big bang without divine intervention of some sort)." One respondent surmised, "Based on the complexity, intricacy, and beauty of the world I don't see how anything could exist without being created." Another respondent was dubious that "life and everything around us came from nothing, by chance, and evolved into present day. Even if the Bible didn't exist, that's a tough sell."

The second category of responses to this question centered on the basis of morality. Many respondents were unconvinced a moral system could develop absent a creator. One participant identified the inherent contradiction in a godless morality: "I generally find [atheistic beliefs] to be logically inconsistent. For example, in a recent conversation a friend ridiculed the belief in God or any absolute basis for morality, yet felt *some* behavior was absolutely immoral."

The final category of responses to this question concerned nihilism, or a felt absence of purpose in a godless reality, i.e., "...that we only have this one life... that there are no miracles of divine power." One respondent expressed doubt "that we just die and that is the end," while another theorized, "I find that atheists struggle when it comes to finding joy in the overall purpose or meaning of life. I find myself longing for meaning and purpose and would struggle with the randomness of nature if it weren't overseen by a sovereign, almighty God."

Pretest Open-Ended Question #3: Which atheistic belief(s), if any, do you find most convincing?

There were 151 responses to this question, concerning the *most* convincing aspects of atheistic belief. Many simply replied they found *no* convincing beliefs in atheism, while a few indicated the challenge inherent in communicating an experience of the divine to those who have had no such experience. "I can't convince someone who doesn't have faith to have faith, it's the work of the Holy Spirit. Just like I can never explain to a Ugandan how wonderful it is to stand outside on a perfect winter day and feel the snow falling… they'll never understand unless they can experience it for themselves - a lot like faith and the goodness of God."

The majority of responses regarding atheism's more convincing tenets break into two categories. First, the validity of scientific thought was expressed by a number of participants: "The scientific explanation for the origin of the world, existence of dinosaurs, and so on." Another response identified a leaning toward "promotion of science as the final say." A third stated, "Doesn't religion seem kind of fantastical? A little hard to believe that people lived to be hundreds of years old or that only one family survived some huge flood."

In addition to scientific thought, the second area of atheistic thought that was most often compelling to respondents regarded the problem of pain. "Why would God allow so much suffering?" asked one participant. "The problem of suffering," said another," is not a convincing point, but is one that can be mysterious and often a challenge to attempt to explain." A third simply stated, "Problem of pain - toughest to respond."

Pretest Open-Ended Question #4:   Any additional comments, recommendations, or suggestions?

For the final pretest question, inviting any additional comments, 92 participants replied. Responses varied broadly and make broad categorization difficult. A number of responses expressed interest in the upcoming sermon series or a desire for the survey results to eventually be made public.

A minority of the responses to this question took the opportunity to express dissatisfaction with the survey in general or concern about the overall objective. One respondent questioned, "Why is this survey not asking what people find most and least convincing about Christianity?" Another stated, "It isn't our job to convince anyone of anything. We should allow God to work in other people's lives and pray that we might be used in whatever he is doing. Going on the offensive is just that – offensive." A third cautioned, "Stop trying to find so many differences and start trying to find similarities between all mankind. These books of parables serve only to divide us (like your survey is trying to do)."

Posttest Open-Ended Question #1: In what way(s), if any, was the recent MCC preaching series "The God Who is There?" most helpful to you?

The posttest survey, following the sermon series, offered three open-ended questions, inviting the participant to reflect on whatever portion of the six-part sermon series they experienced. For the first question which inquired what portion of the series, if any, was helpful, 81 responses were submitted. Many of the comments noted appreciation for a clear and well researched presentation, mentioned the series confirmed already held beliefs, or referenced the emphasis on functional atheism: "The repetitive re-statements of truths replaced by un-truths provided good review and were helpful for knowledge retention; the discussion about functional atheism was convicting and instructional."

Several respondents indicated the usefulness of being exposed to atheistic dogma, some for the first time: "It outlined the major beliefs of atheists which I did not know," one stated. Another offered, "I liked that the series oriented outward, so to speak… The sermon series challenged you to get out from under your fear and intellectual laziness and understand what's going on in our culture."

Finally, not all respondents found the series of use. When replying to what was most helpful, one respondent tersely offered, "not much." Another respondent stated, "Wanted to see how it represented atheism, and how it dealt with the arguments… I was curious to see if he could make a convincing argument that could make me pause to reconsider (or at least re-examine) my current beliefs (generally atheist/agnostic). In the end there was nothing presented that challenged my disbelief."

Posttest Open-Ended Question #2: In what way(s), if any, could the recent MCC preaching series "The God Who is There" have been more helpful? What constructive criticism can you offer?

When invited to identify ways the preaching series could be improved, 66 individuals offered responses (although several of these responses indicated "none" or "n/a"). Some respondents suggested they would be helped by additional Scriptures being referenced, others mentioned the lecture style was "impressive but complicated." At least two respondents believed the series improved after the first week or two. For instance, one respondent stated, "Some parts during the 1st and 2nd sermon were very heady." Another reflected, "The first sermon left me a little too empty.

Maybe it was just me, or maybe there was not enough hope in Jesus at the end of the sermon. I'm not sure. But the last four certainly gave me firm ground to stand on when I left the sanctuary."

The most frequent piece of constructive criticism centered around the question of whether a sermon series is the best vehicle to tackle a subject like Christian engagement with atheism. "While the Romans passage was well explained and preached, seemed like the seminar approach would have been more helpful as a class than as a sermon series."

Posttest Open-Ended Question #3: Any additional comments, recommendations, or suggestions?

The final open ended question on the posttest netted no particularly new insights. A number of encouragements and notes of appreciation for the series were offered, for instance, "All in all I thought it was a great series and very interesting, especially having two children who have walked away from their faith. The suppress statements really stand out." Some respondents reiterated the series may work better as a class or forum rather than a sermon series. Others noted their appreciation for the unusual, change-of-pace type teaching: "It might have been out of the congregation's comfort zone, but it should be done occasionally to teach the modern day challenges that Christians must face."

Conclusion
Project Critique and Future Research

A Critique of the Project Design

Overall, it would appear the pretest and posttest surveys were, in concert with the intervening sermon series, effectively designed to accomplish set goals. The surveys allowed the researcher to measure thoughts and opinions related to atheism, and then measure how, if at all, the six-part sermon series impacted those views. A professional marketing and analysis company was able to confirm that survey results were well designed to net statistically significant results.

Although the project's overall objectives were accomplished, this is not to say improvements to the project could not be made for a future iteration. One area of minor improvement on the pretest would be the inclusion of "retired" and "unemployed" categories under the demographics question about career. In addition, the inclusion of the "understanding atheist's views on science" question, on the pretest, would allow for a pretest/posttest comparison of the results.

Regarding the sermon series, feedback from the congregation was primarily positive and the researcher's own self-assessment suggests the sermons were well constructed. However, within the series, sermons 1 and 2 were consistently viewed as the weakest of the set. Improvement could be made to tighten these early sermon's presentations rather than overwhelming the listener with facts, figures, and academic quotations.

Moving to a higher-level critique of the project, a larger sampling of various ethnicities would make the overall results far more powerful. Ethnic diversity was difficult to accomplish in a Boston Metrowest context where the population is primarily Caucasian. Related to this issue of racial diversity was the small sample size from regions outside New England. A repeat of the project design, in a different area of the country with more ethnic diversity, may result in alternate and intriguing results.

Perhaps the most challenging aspect of the project implementation was the change from a religiously broader pretest population (9% non-Christian) to a much narrower, posttest population (only 2% non-Christian). Even when demographically filtering test results, it was not always clear how the different, religious affiliations between test populations impacted overall results. The challenge, of course, is how can one move a significant number of non-Christians, without overwhelming attrition, through a multi-week sermon series on atheism to eventually allow for posttesting?

Possibilities for Future Research

The project design and implementation described in chapters 4 and 5 have led to compelling questions that invite future study. Alluded to in the previous section, the inclusion of additional ethnicities and regions of the country would allow for a sharpening of the preaching material. Feedback from a more racially diverse population could likely assist in the formulation of effective discipleship materials to train evangelical Christians how to humbly and graciously engage with an atheistic worldview.

A consistent result, on both the pretest and posttest, was the tendency for men to rate their understanding of atheistic dogma significantly higher than women rated their own understanding. *Why is this? Does the difference in perceived understanding have an actual basis in reality, or are males simply predisposed to artificially inflate their perception of familiarity with atheism?*

Another consistent result, on both the pretest and posttest, was the tendency for the age 18-29 bracket to lag significantly behind older age-groups regarding confidence in the Bible's ability to answer atheism. Although the posttest sample size was small, this younger age bracket was also less predisposed to avail themselves of sermon teaching on the topic. An unsurprising corollary to these findings was that the 18-29 bracket is significantly more likely to *personally* lean toward atheistic convictions regardless of *public*, religious affiliation. Countless books and articles have been written on the millennial generation's drift from Christian orthodoxy and ecclesiastical connection. However, focused testing upon the 18-29 group and adaptation of the current project design specifically for this bracket could be beneficial.

Finally, Pew, Barna and numerous other groups have completed helpful studies to explore atheism as a subset of the religiously non-affiliated. However, a largely untapped area of research concerns the dissemination of atheistic concepts to those who label themselves theistic. *How do atheistic dogmas, uncovered in the present study, trickle into the larger, public consciousness? How can Christians be better equipped for defense against atheistic principles cloaked in seemingly non-religious contexts?* Research around these questions, and the answers such research produces, may significantly impact the American churches viability – or lack thereof – for generations to come.

APPENDIX A
Pretest Survey

ENGAGING WITH ATHEISM: A Research Project Survey

Welcome!

Thank you for participating in the following survey which comprises a portion of the research for my doctoral studies; your time is greatly appreciated. The following survey is broken into three, brief sections with multiple choice options. The fourth and final section is composed of a few, *optional* questions that allow for open-ended response.

Total time to complete the survey will be approximately 5 to 6 minutes. All data submitted is SSL encrypted and completely anonymous. The survey can be completed using either desktop or mobile devices.

Please click the button below to begin...

Sincerely,
Travis Bond

ENGAGING WITH ATHEISM: A Research Project Survey

Section 1 of 4: Demographic Information (7 Questions)

* 1. Are you male or female?

    ◯ Male

    ◯ Female

* 2. What is your age range?

    ◯ under 18

    ◯ 18-29

    ◯ 30-39

    ◯ 40-49

    ◯ 50-64

    ◯ 65+

* 3. How do you describe your race?

○ American Indian or Alaskan Native

○ Asian

○ Black or African American

○ Latino

○ White or Caucasian

○ Some other race (please specify)

[_____]

* 4. In what area of the United States do you currently reside?

○ New England

○ Mid-Atlantic

○ South

○ South-West

○ Mid-West

○ Pacific States

○ Some other region or a different country (please specify)

[_____]

* 5. What is the highest level of education you have completed or the highest degree you have received?

○ Less than high school degree

○ High school degree or equivalent (e.g., GED)

○ Associate degree

○ Bachelor degree

○ Masters Degree

○ Doctoral Degree

* 6. Which of the following best describes your religious affiliation?

○ Agnostic

○ Atheist

○ Buddhist

○ Christian

○ Hindu

○ Jewish

○ Muslim

○ No affiliation

○ Other (please specify)

[   ]

* 7. Which of the following best describes your current job?

○ For-profit organization

○ Full-time homemaker

○ Nonprofit organization

○ Student

○ Unemployed

○ Other (please specify)

[   ]

ENGAGING WITH ATHEISM: A Research Project Survey

Section 2 of 4: Social Engagement with Atheism (7 Questions)

* 8. To the best of my knowledge, I often engage in day-to-day conversation with atheists*(regarding work, marriage, parenting, politics, etc):*

strongly disagree	tend to disagree	neutral	tend to agree	strongly agree	I Don't Know
○	○	○	○	○	○

* 9. To the best of my knowledge, I often engage in spiritual conversation with atheists *(regarding eternity, personal faith, the way faith interacts with everyday issues, etc)*:

strongly disagree	tend to disagree	neutral	tend to agree	strongly agree	I Don't Know
○	○	○	○	○	○

* 10. I feel well equipped to explain and defend my religious faith in conversation with an atheist:

strongly disagree	tend to disagree	neutral	tend to agree	strongly agree	I Don't Know
○	○	○	○	○	○

* 11. I believe atheism is an increasing demographic in the region where I reside:

strongly disagree	tend to disagree	neutral	tend to agree	strongly agree	I Don't Know
○	○	○	○	○	○

* 12. I believe atheism is an increasing demographic throughout the United States:

strongly disagree	tend to disagree	neutral	tend to agree	strongly agree	I Don't Know
○	○	○	○	○	○

* 13. I believe atheism is an increasing demographic worldwide:

strongly disagree	tend to disagree	neutral	tend to agree	strongly agree	I Don't Know
○	○	○	○	○	○

* 14. I believe present-day atheists are increasingly outspoken when compared to atheists 20 years ago:

strongly disagree	tend to disagree	neutral	tend to agree	strongly agree	I Don't Know
○	○	○	○	○	○

ENGAGING WITH ATHEISM: A Research Project Survey

Section 3 of 4: Personal Engagement with Atheism (4 Questions)

* 15. I have a good understanding of the atheistic world and life view*(e.g. general atheistic beliefs)*:

strongly disagree	tend to disagree	neutral	tend to agree	strongly agree
○	○	○	○	○

* 16. I have a good understanding of how atheists view the basis of morality:

strongly disagree	tend to disagree	neutral	tend to agree	strongly agree
○	○	○	○	○

* 17. I have a good understanding of how atheists view the origin of the universe:

strongly disagree	tend to disagree	neutral	tend to agree	strongly agree
○	○	○	○	○

* 18. I have a good understanding of how atheists view the purpose of human life:

strongly disagree	tend to disagree	neutral	tend to agree	strongly agree
○	○	○	○	○

* 19. I believe the Christian Bible offers a convincing response to an atheistic understanding of reality:

strongly disagree	tend to disagree	neutral	tend to agree	strongly agree
○	○	○	○	○

* 20. Regardless of my publicly stated religion, I increasingly lean toward atheism as my own personal conviction:

strongly disagree	tend to disagree	neutral	tend to agree	strongly agree
○	○	○	○	○

ENGAGING WITH ATHEISM: A Research Project Survey

Section 4 of 4: Optional Responses (4 Questions)

21. In what way(s), if any, would you like to be better equipped to defend your religious faith while in conversation with an atheist?

22. Which atheistic belief(s), if any, do you find least convincing?

146

WEEK 1 OF 6: INCONVENIENT TRUTH
Romans 1:18

The Big Idea: A suppression of truth inevitably leads to fragmented lives.

Introduction

A. Pastor Carl and I were having our weekly meeting last Thursday where we always meet, at the local saloon, when he made a staggering claim to me: *"Trav, I don't think Kentucky actually exists."* *"What?"* I replied. *"What are you talking about?"*

- *"I'm a skeptic,"* he explained, *"A cynic. A doubter. An A-Kentuckian if you will."*

- *"Carl,"* I said, *"I think you've been working too hard. This doesn't make any sense."*

- *"Think about it Trav. The whole thing is a conspiracy to drum up tourism. All that talk about Abraham Lincoln, Shawnee Indians. None of its real."*

B. At this point I just stared at him for a moment...as Neil Diamond's *Kentucky Woman* began playing over the radio. *"Carl, you realize our own Assistant Pastor went to seminary there."*

- *"Honestly Trav, does Don seem that educated to you?"*

- *"Hmm – fair point. But what about The Kentucky Derby, Kentucky Fried Chicken, Kentucky Wildcats, Daniel Boone, and millions of people claim to have been born in the state. I mean, if you don't believe it exists, where's your evidence?"*

- *"Ahh,"* Carl replied knowingly, *"I see your problem."*

- *"My problem."*

- *"Yes. Your confusion actually. You see Trav, you think my denial of Kentucky is a claim of some kind. A belief. It is not. It's actually a non-belief. I'm talking about something I lack – namely belief in a state where grass is supposedly blue. I don't need to give evidence."*

- *"You don't?!"* I asked. *"Listen, Trav. You don't give evidence for non-belief in unicorns, leprechauns, or the Customer Support Department at Verizon. None of those things are real. In the same way, I'm not making a claim. I'm making a non-claim. I'm rejecting a belief. And I don't have to prove a negative. Now, please quit arguing and pour me another shot of Kentucky Bourbon."*

C. You know, if there is one sphere in which our atheist friends most pride themselves, it is the embrace of eminently rationalistic thought. *"Atheism is for thinking people."* Much is made of even having a term like a-theist or non-theist. Many prefer the term "Brights" instead. No one identifies themselves as a non-astrologer, or a non-alchemist, so what need exists, the atheist asks, to label with a negative.

- It's a compelling argument, right up until you substitute the existence of Kentucky for the existence of God. Because when you do that, it becomes quite obvious there are categories of both belief and non-belief that DO require evidence.
- My name is Travis Bond, I serve as the Senior Pastor here, and we're starting this morning a six-part series titled, "The God Who is There." This is gonna be kind of a 30,000 foot flyover of some key concepts, how those concepts affect the larger culture, and then finally how the church can respond with grace.

I Why This Study?

A. Now If you are brand new this morning, I kinda want you to know this is not normal. I am very committed to expository preaching as the steady diet of the church. Even when I do topical sermons like this, I usually expound a specific text. Now we're still gonna be anchored in the Scripture this morning, but we're coming at it from a different angle in this series. But why? Why atheism?

- I mean, I have no interest in doing a sermon series on where we disagree with our Muslim friends, or our Hindu friends. I'm preaching no sermons on why we're not Mormons, or Scientologists. So why a series on the topic of atheism?
- Back in 2013, when this church (that I love so much) offered to support my work toward a doctorate, I committed in my own mind that whenever I could, I wanted to chase research projects that could directly serve this local church. And I've come to the conviction MCC is gonna be facing two cultural waves we really need to understand. The first one is our nation's radical change in sexual ethics. *"What is happening? Eoes the Bible speak to it?"* You'll recall we spent about nine months unpacking that as a church family, which included a four-part sermon series.

- Beyond sexual ethics, a second cultural wave washing over the church today, looks like this. And this. And this. According to Pew Research, 20% of our population now self-identifies as no religious affiliation. In 1990, 8.1% of Americans were religiously non-affiliated. 25 year later, that number is over 20%. This is called the Rise of the Nones.
- Now check it out, this is the one that should blow your mind. Among those age 18-29, that non-affiliated number was 32% in 2012. The percentage went up 4% in two years. Within our increasingly-similar-to-Europe, post-Christian context, there is a seismic shift occurring in religious views and religious affiliation.

B. Now let me be clear, when folks check off the box "no-affiliation" on religious surveys, that is not synonymous with atheism. About 27% of Nones also self-describe as atheist. Most of the other non-affiliated describe themselves as theistic, agnostic (not sure about the existence of God) or believe in a universal spirit of some sort. And yet none of them want to join with religious institutions. Which means they possess:

- Minimal Biblical doctrine – Minimal church history – Minimal spiritual accountability.
- And here's my thesis: this rise of the Nones has been dramatically influenced and encouraged by the advent of what we call New Atheism. Which exploded right about here **<laser pointer graph>**

C. I had a presentation on this at last year's *Christ & Culture Conference*. Lot of you were here so I'll just do the Cliff's Notes. New Atheism is a term coined by Wired Magazine back in 2006. New Atheism is old atheism repackaged. Guys like Bertrand Russell, Sigmund Freud, Charles Darwin. It's their same atheistic concepts, but repackaged with a sometimes angry, often brash, always militant attitude. For instance, here's Richard Dawkins – the most widely recognized New Atheist – in his own words. This was several years ago at a Ted conference. **<Militant Atheism Video>**

- Richard Dawkins is one of the self-titled "Four Horsemen of the Non-Apocalypse." These are the most well-known, identifiable faces of New Atheism.
    1. You've got Dawkins, an Oxford Biologist wrote a book titled *The God Delusion* which has sold millions and millions of copies.
    2. Christopher Hitchens, now deceased, was an author and journalist who wrote *God is Not Great: Why Religion Poisons Everything*.
    3. Sam Harris, a neuroscientist, wrote *The End of Faith: Religion, Terror, and the Future of Reason*.

4. And Daniel Dennett, right here in Boston is a professor of Philosophy at Tufts and wrote *Breaking the Spell: Religion as a Natural Phenomenon.*

C. We'll be getting to know these guys a bit more. They're all prolific writers. But <u>why</u> do they write? Well, Dawkins puts it like this:

"If this book works as intended, religious readers who open it will be atheists when they put it down. What presumptuous optimism! Of course, dyed-in-the-wool faith-heads are immune to argument, their resistance built up over years of childhood indoctrination using methods that took centuries to mature."

- Now, that's a pretty clever paragraph. *"If you read my book, I trust you'll convert to Atheism. But if you don't, it's because you're an idiot. Or at least a religiously brainwashed cretin."*
- Well, <u>my</u> goal in this sermon-series is a bit more modest. If you are a self-described atheist (and by the way we have several who regularly attend our services), if you are an atheist or a curious unbeliever, I have two goals. To borrow from a Brit named Andy Bannister:
  1. I hope you'll be a bit more of a thought-through atheist or unbeliever. Maybe a doubter rather than a skeptic.
  2. And secondly, I hope you'll be a bit more trusting that Christians really are trying to use our brains just like you.
- If you're a Christian, two goals as well. More familiar with atheism:
  1. So you can understand both its, strengths and its weaknesses – thereby strengthening your own faith.
  2. Understand the ranting of the New Atheists is one <u>segment</u> of atheism. There are many more fair, open-minded atheists who are friendly, good-humored, they want community, and they appreciate honest dialogue. Hopefully, in the weeks ahead, you'll be a little more confident <u>having</u> that dialogue.

II Atheistic Attacks

A. So where does all this touch down in Scripture? Well, there's a lot of places we <u>could</u> go. But maybe the best place, and the spot where we <u>will</u> go, is the New Testament Book of Romans, chapter 1. If you have you're Bibles, go ahead and open up to Romans, this is page 939 in the pew Bibles. For the next few weeks, this is where we drop anchor. We're gonna key in on ten verses, and that will be the spine of our study. We'll branch off from here into various spots, but we'll keep coming home to Romans 1. Let me read the first five verses of this passage. Romans 1, beginning at verse 16:

16 For I am not ashamed of the gospel, because it is the power of God that brings salvation to everyone who believes: first to the Jew, then to the Gentile. **17** For in the gospel the righteousness of God is revealed—a righteousness that is by faith from first to last, just as it is written: "The righteous will live by faith. **18** The wrath of God is being revealed from heaven against all the godlessness and wickedness of people, who suppress the truth by their wickedness. **19** For what can be known about God is plain to them, because God has shown it to them. **20** For his invisible attributes, namely, his eternal power and divine nature, have been clearly perceived, ever since the creation of the world, in the things that have been made. So they are without excuse.

B. You know, Mark Twain once stated that *"heaven is for climate, hell is for society."* Which is a good line. That passing, somewhat amused view of religion was once prominent in atheism. The tide has turned. New Atheism seeks to reduce, embarrass, and dismiss religion.

- Dawkins: *"The atonement, the central doctrine of Christianity, [is] vicious, sado-masochistic and repellent. We should also dismiss it as barking mad, but for its ubiquitous familiarity which has dulled our objectivity."*

- Harris: *"We have names for people who have many beliefs for which there is no rational justification. When their beliefs are extremely common we call them 'religious'; otherwise, they are likely to be called 'mad', 'psychotic' or 'delusional'."*

- Seth Andrews, a radio personality: *"Ignorance is celebrated. Curiosity is quelled. Fear is cultivated. Science is largely distrusted. And brainwashed individuals struggle to make sense of their own lives as they frantically struggle to pound the square peg of religion into the round hole of reason."*

II The Suppression of Truth
A. So condescending mocking of Christianity is nothing new. Although it was not previously so acceptable. But here's the question that interests

me – and the state of Kentucky: If God is really there, why would he display anger toward those who deny truth. , Verse 18: "who by their unrighteousness suppress the truth."

- Does that sound odd to you that we have a moral imperative to know something? Consider – in a court of law you solemnly swear to say everything you know about the topic at hand.   The branch of philosophy that focuses on knowledge is called epistemology. And Nancy Pearcey says we have an epistemic duty to acknowledge what we know and conform our lives to it. In other words, at the heart of the human condition is an epistemological sin: the refusal to acknowledge what can be known about God.

- That's what verse 18 and following is talking about.   By our unrighteousness we suppress the truth. *"There comes a moment,"* C.S. Lewis once wrote, *"when the children who have been playing at burglars hush suddenly: was that a real footstep in the hall? There comes a moment when people who have been dabbling in religion suddenly draw back. Supposing we really found Him?"*

C. So whether you believe it or not, here's what the Bible is saying. All forms of unbelief, which include Atheism, are truth-suppression. Now if you're non-religious, here's how you might counter: *"Okay Trav, if that's accurate, if in my "sinful" heart I am suppressing the truth of God – wouldn't that truth somehow leak out on the edges."* Glad you asked. And you're exactly right. See, the way a worldview is tested in real time is by moving out of a two-story, existence. Stepping out of the classroom and into life. Can a Godless worldview be lived consistently without God leaking out at the edges?   Does life function the way your worldview says it should? Does it fit reality?

- See, if Paul's thesis is correct, and men by their unrighteousness suppress what is true, that flawed worldview would show cracks. True <u>truth</u> keeps bubbling to the surface.

- Would it surprise you to learn, in their more authentic moments, multiple atheists have confessed a disconnect between what they profess and what they feel. Dr. Paul Davis, respected cosmologist at the University of Arizona:

"Can the mighty edifice of physical order we perceive in the world about us ultimately be rooted in reasonless absurdity? If so, then nature is a fiendishly clever bit of trickery: meaninglessness and absurdity somehow

masquerading as ingenious order and rationality."

- Cognitive scientist Edward Slingerland, in a section of his book ironically titled *We are Robots Designed Not to Believe that We are Robots*:

"We need to pull off the trick of living with a <u>dual consciousness</u>, cultivating the ability to view human beings simultaneously under two descriptions: as physical systems and as person."

- Rodley Brooks, from right here at MIT:
"When I look at my children, I can, when I force myself ... see that they are machines ... That is not how I treat them ... I maintain two sets of <u>inconsistent beliefs</u>."

D. Folks, this is an important point: when someone talks about concepts they believe to be <u>untrue</u>, yet those same concepts are vital for a humane social order, that is a strong indicator you've bumped up against the edge of a reality that does not fit your worldview. "Men, who by their unrighteousness suppress truth" are living a two story, bi-polar existence.

- Here's Slingerland again:

"the idea of my daughter as merely a complex robot carrying my genes into the next generation is both bizarre and repugnant to me... There may well be individuals who lack this sense, and who can quite easily and thoroughly conceive of themselves and other people in purely instrumental, mechanistic terms, but we label such people 'psychopaths,' and quite rightly try to identify them and put them away somewhere to protect the rest of us."

- Does thus fit reality? Should someone who <u>correctly</u> <u>understands</u> human existence be labeled a psychopath?
- Here's what it all means: atheists, just like the rest of us apart from knowing God, live fragmented, schizophrenic lives. Choosing month after month and year after year, to disbelieve what is obvious and apparent – that is the definition of truth suppression.

Conclusion

A. And so all that really takes us back to the existence of Kentucky. Should non-belief offer evidence? Is A-theist a fair term? Here's Dawkins once again. **<Teapot Agnostic Video>**

- Dawkins is a brilliant man. Smarter than I'll ever be. But very smart people are sometimes very wrong. Both beliefs and non-beliefs, deserve to be defended. Because truth, this is important, truth always leads to trust.

- It's what Romans 1:18 is about. It's what this table is about. The Lord's supper is for those who have reached the end of themselves, who are tired of suppressing what is true, and are prepared to rest by faith in the one said, *"I am the way, and the truth, and the life."* Carl?

> **The Big Idea:** To show the listener how ignoring revelation and embracing materialism leads to emptiness and contradiction.

"The Hook"

A. So last week Pastor Carl and I were relaxing at the beach – as we often do – in April – after it snows. Beach chairs fully reclined, sunning ourselves, skin of winter white gleaming forth when suddenly a little brother and sister in swimsuits ran up to us in a panic. *"Hey misters, you're pastors right?"* We are of course used to this sort of thing happening. We give off a pastor vibe. It's kinda like being a superhero – but with male pattern balding.

- *"Yes, little children.,"* I replied. *"We are pastors. How may we pastorally assist you."*
- *"We lost our rubber duckie,"* they cried. *"Will you help us find it?"*
- At this point, I did what most anyone would do in my situation. I pointed to Pastor Carl and said, *"actually, he's the nice one."*

B. As you might guess, in no time at all Pastor Carl leapt to action. *"Don't worry kids,"* he declared, *"I have just the thing."* Immediately Carl bent over, reached into his floral-print beach bag, and pulled out a telescoping metal detector.

- Before I could say a word, the wand was extended, headphones were on, and Carl was off – combing the sand. (That's an actual picture. Carl looks older on the beach).
- Would you believe Pastor Carl spent hours in the sand, with his metal detector, searching for the rubber duckie.
- As the sun dropped low, Carl reported back to the small children. *"Sorry kids; spare change, aluminum cans, Rolex watch. But there is nothing on that beach made of rubber."* So with heads down and shoulders slumped, the two little children walked away dejectedly.

C. Afterwards, I said to Carl, *"I really admired your enthusiasm in the rubber duckie search, but are you sure you used the right tool?"*

- *"Absolutely,"* Carl replied. *"I searched everywhere with this thing. There is nothing made of rubber out there. Or plastic for that matter. Or wood. In fact, I double-checked in the parking lot and the boardwalk and the bathrooms. I'm wondering if rubber, plastic, and wood are actually a myth altogether."* Meanwhile I couldn't help notice his metal detector was mostly made of rubber and plastic, with a wooden handle.

- You know, in a sense, atheism is a lot like metal-detector man and science becomes the metal detector. Not that atheists are unintelligent. Certainly not. We have several who regularly attend MCC. And science is amazing. It is absolutely amazing at discovering natural causes in the natural world. But much like the man with a hammer to whom everything is a nail, if you're only equipped to discover material things, material things is all you'll ever discover.

Introduction

A. My name is Travis Bond, I serve as Senior Pastor here, and this morning is part two of a six part series we're calling *The God Who Is There: A Study on Faith and Unbelief.* If you have your Bibles, please open up to our anchor passage in the New Testament book of Romans, chapter 1. If you're using one of the Black Bibles this is p939. Romans 1 is the spine of our six week study. We'll follow some connective tissue now and then, but we're gonna keep coming back to Romans 1 which offers this incredible dissection or autopsy on unbelief.

- Warning, big word: If epistemology means the study of knowledge – how we know what we know – then last week we spent a lot of time unpacking how at the heart of the human condition lies an epistemological sin. You, me, atheists, deists, muslims, Buddhists – everybody on the planet is predisposed to suppress truth. That's part of living in a fallen world. Sin suppresses truth.
- That leads us to the thesis of this sermon series: every time you suppress a truth, an untruth will fill its place. **Repeat.** Nature abhors a vacuum.

B. So in our anchor passage, this reality is set forth in each and every verse. Whenever you suppress a truth, you have to put an untruth in its place. We're working through a ten verse passage, I'm gonna read just five verses this morning, our attention will be on verses 19 & 20. So as I read this, see if you can spot the epistemological error. In other words, what is the truth being suppressed and what is the untruth offered in its place? Romans 1, beginning at verse 16, this is the very Word of the Lord.

16 I am not ashamed of the gospel, for it is the power of God for salvation to everyone who believes, to the Jew first and also to the Greek. **17** For in it the righteousness of God is revealed from faith for faith, as it is written, "The righteous shall live by faith." **18** For the wrath of God is revealed from heaven against all ungodliness and unrighteousness of men, who by their unrighteousness <u>suppress the truth</u>. **19** For what can be known about God is plain to them, because God has shown it to them. **20** For his invisible attributes, namely, his eternal power and divine nature, have been <u>clearly perceived</u>, ever since the creation of the world, <u>in the things that have been made</u>. So they are without excuse.

I Materialism Introduced

A. Why are we doing a sermon series on belief and unbelief and atheism? If you're a guest this morning, I almost never preach this way – the seminar style. This is an unusual series, it's a bit more heady (I know that), but you're a really bright congregation and I'm convinced, even if we have to stretch our minds a little here, Romans 1 is really important because – *the times they are a changin'.*

- Listen, God will get the victory. God will always get the victory. Historical trends will go up, they will go down yet Christ will build his church and the gates of hell will not prevail. That's the big picture.

- Sometimes it's hard to see the big picture. You and I are living at a time where in the global north and in the United States, religious <u>non</u>-affiliation is sharply rising. And this trend, particularly since the mid-2000's, is correlated with the rise of something called *New Atheism.* Championed by men like Dawkins, Hitchens, Harris, and Dennett, New Atheism is a repackaging of old atheism in a much more brash, much more militant style.

- Now self-labeled atheists make up a small percentage of the American population – 3.1%. Agnostics add another 4%. But New Atheism ideas, and increasingly their style, have an outsized influence. In your child's school. In your entertainment. In your state house. And to a massive degree, the university.

B. Here's this morning's big idea: *"Materialism masks what Creation conveys."* **Repeat.** Now when we use this word "materialism" in church, usually we're talking about being consumeristic. Greedy, materialistic, focused on getting stuff. This morning, I'm using this word in the scientific sense.

- Materialism is a philosophical position that says all things – every thing – can be reduced to matter. What is ultimately real – in fact, the only thing that is real – is molecules in motion. Everything can be reduced to that.
- Now think it through – what's the intellectual problem with this position? Well it's self-defeating. Frank Turek says, *"analyzing atheist claims is like trying to gargle peanut butter…if everyone is a molecular machine, why do atheists act as if they can freely and reasonably arrive at atheistic conclusions?"*
- Do you follow? If there's no such thing as soul, or spirit, or consciousness or divinely ordained absolutes – if it's only neurons firing and molecules moving, what makes your conclusions dreamed up in a random, material-only brain, valid? And why does it even matter?

C. In the text on your lap, verse 19, Paul's introducing a theological category we call "natural revelation." Have you guys heard of that before? Special revelation is God's revealing himself to us through his Word. The Bible. That's the only way we know redemption through Christ; special revelation. Natural Revelation is everything else.

> **1** The heavens declare the glory of God, and the sky above proclaims his handiwork.
> **2** Day to day pours out speech, and night to night reveals knowledge.

- That's Psalm 19. Well our Romans 1 text is saying the exact same thing. Verse 19 again: What can be known about God is plain … his invisible attributes … his eternal power and divine nature, have been clearly perceived, ever since the creation of the world, in the things that have been made.
- To quote a biologist named Ariel Roth: *"God never performed a miracle to convince an atheist, because His ordinary works provide sufficient evidence."*

II Materialism Answered

A. Now you guys know these things. You may not think in terms of the category "natural revelation," but most of us have said things along these lines. *"Trav, when I look at the stars, when I look at a newborn baby, the*

intricacy of nature I don't understand how someone can deny a designer."
And that's exactly right.

- The problem is that cannot be empirically tested. You cannot run a material test for non-material things. Therefore, most atheists accept a worldview which says only material things exist. Metal is all the metal detector ever found. Get it? *"Materialism masks what creation conveys."* The power and splendor and majesty of the God who is there.
- Materialists live and look in one category – the empirically tested universe. They treat matter and energy as the only things real, knowable and and objectively true. Therefore, pushed up into the attic, the upper story, is everything that does not fit the naturalist box – soul, objective morality, love, eternal purpose.

B. C.S. Lewis identified the self-defeating nature of materialism.

> *"If minds are wholly dependent on brains, and brains on biochemistry, and biochemistry (in the long run) on the meaningless flux of the atoms, I cannot understand how the thought of those minds should have any more significance than the sound of the wind in the trees."*

- In other words, individuals who cannot trust their own objectively true thinking cannot trust the arguments leading to atheism – which leaves them little reason to be atheists. The whole thing becomes gargling peanut butter.
- John Lennox is a professor of mathematics at the University of Oxford. Brilliant man. I heard him speak a few years ago. His daughter, incidentally, is the one who does our Getty Hymns. *In Christ Alone, O Church Arise.* Anyway, Dr. Lennox writes:

> *"[according to atheism] the mind that does science ... is the end product of a mindless unguided process. Now, if you knew your computer was the product of a mindless unguided process, you wouldn't trust it. So, to me atheism undermines the rationality I need to do science."*

C. That's a pretty solid point. So how do our atheist friends respond? Honestly, they don't. It's a lot like the relativist who proclaims all truth is relative, there are no absolutes – except for my conviction that all truth is relative there are no absolutes. That's absolute. In one form or another, atheists all do that – they make a tacit exception for their beliefs, trusting their own thinking as reliable – despite its origin in a mindless, unguided process. Atheists always exempt themselves from the despair of their own conclusions. They have to.

- But then, every now and then (and I read a lot of these guys) you come across a brilliant person who admits – accidentally or not – what's really going on. Here's geneticist and avowed atheist Richard Lewontin, professor at Harvard:

"It is not that the methods and institutions of science somehow compel us to accept a material explanation ... but on the contrary we are forced by our a priori adherence to material causes to create an apparatus of investigation and a set of concepts that produce material explanation, no matter how counter-intuitive .... materialism is an absolute for we cannot allow a Divine Foot in the door."

- Translation: we will only use a metal detector on the beach. We refuse from the outset to consider the possibility that rubber, plastic, or wood could be on the beach. And shockingly, we've never found rubber, plastic, or wood.

D. Materialists are like the drunk guy who thinks his care keys must be under the lamp-post because that's the only place where there's light to look. And he refuses to listen to those who found them elsewhere.

- "Materialism masks what Creation conveys." When you suppress the truth of Creation, it's replaced with the untruth that physical matter is all there is. 1 Corinthians 1:

"Where is the one who is wise? Where is the scribe? Where is the debater of this age? Has not God made foolish the wisdom of the world? "

Conclusion

A. Dawkins tells how in a desert plain in Tanzania, there's a dune made of volcanic ash. The beautiful thing is that it moves bodily. It's known as a "barchan," and the entire dune walks across the desert in a westerly direction at a speed of about 55 feet per year. It retains its crescent shape and moves in the direction of the horns. What happens is that the wind blows the sand up the shallow slope on the outside, then as each grain hits the top of the ridge, it cascades down the inside of the crescent; thus the whole dune gradually moves.

- Now you and I, we are more like that sand dune than we might admit. Think of an experience from your childhood, something you remember clearly, something you can see, feel, maybe even smell, as if you were really there. After all, you really were there weren't you? How else would you remember it? But here's the bombshell: You weren't there. Not a single atom that is in your body today was there when that event took place. Folks, whatever we are, it is more than what we are made of.
- God invites us, in Christ, to know more than what can seen in a telescope or perceived in a microscope or found with a metal detector. You, my friend, are body and soul, precious to the Lord of creation.
- So resist, and teach your children to resist, the lie that this is all we are. You are made in the image of God. You bear the fingerprints of the Creator.

O Lord my God, when I in awesome wonder,
Consider all the works Thy hands have made;
I see the stars, I hear the rolling thunder,
Thy power throughout the universe displayed.

Then sings my soul, my Savior God, to Thee,
How great Thou art! How great Thou art!

> **The Big Idea:** Science can tell you what you're made of, it can never tell you what you *are*.

The Hook

A. Good morning, my name is Travis Bond, I serve as Senior Pastor here. Spring break so office was quiet this week. Jen's on maternity leave. Cathy's on vacation. Pastor Carl and Jean flew to Europe where they're visiting with Annika. But you guys know Carl. He still calls me every day. Just to chat.

- So the other day I asked him, *"Hey Carl, how's the trip going?"*
- *"Trav,"* he said, *"This hotel is amazing. To my room, they brought both my favorite coffee and favorite oatmeal* (Carl loves oatmeal)*."*
- *"No kidding,"* I said, *"that's fun."*
- *"That's just the start of it,"* he said.   *"They also had books from my favorite authors laid out. Tim Keller, John Piper, and Oprah Winfrey."*
- *"Did they really?"* I said.
- *"And get this, they brought me a selection of my favorite pies after dinner* (Carl loves pie*). They stocked my favorite moisturizer creams.* (Carl <u>loves</u> his moisturizers). *Perfectly sized slippers. And hanging on the wall,"* he said, *"was a fitted terry-cloth robe with a note, 'to my wonderful husband Carl, I hope you enjoy your favorite things.' Can you believe that, Trav? What are the chances? <u>My</u> name is Carl!"*

B. *"Wow,"* I replied, *"Jean sure did a lot of prep."* And then there was silence on the other end. *"Uh, Trav, Jean didn't set all this up. She's never even been to Italy."*

- *"Right, but ... she called all that stuff ahead, don't you think?"*
- *"Trav,"* Carl replied, *"come on. When you add up all the centuries with all the hotels, and all the hotel guests, it was just a matter of time till stuff like this came together by chance. I doubt Jean magically designed all that. It just so happens it all perfectly came together for me! But listen, I gotta go, this phone call is costing me a fortune. And Oprah's book club is calling my name..."*

Introduction

A. Now in that little story, Carl and I were both considering the same evidence, yet arrived at dramatically different conclusions. Why? If you have your Bibles, would you open up to the New Testament book of Romans, chapter 1. Romans chapter 1, this is page 939 in the Black Bibles.

- This morning we're in part three of a six-part series we're calling *"The God Who is There: A Study on Belief and Unbelief."*

- If you're a first-time guest, I want you to know this is a very different kind of series than I usually preach. It's more topical, more heady, more seminar-ish than typical. But what we're seeking to do is better understand atheism. Specifically, how is <u>New</u> Atheism — which is just a brash, militant repackaging of regular old atheism — how is New Atheism influencing culture? And, how might Christians graciously, clearly, and humbly respond?

B. Our anchor passage, or the spine of this series, is Romans 1; I'm gonna read about six verses this morning. We'll start at v16, but our focus will be v21. Follow along with me, this now is the very Word of the Lord:

16 I am <u>NOT ashamed</u> of the gospel, for it is the power of God for salvation to everyone who believes, to the Jew first and also to the Greek. **17** For in it the righteousness of God is revealed from faith for faith, as it is written, "The righteous shall live by faith." **18** For the wrath of God is revealed from heaven against all ungodliness and unrighteousness of men, who by their unrighteousness suppress the truth. **19** For what can be known about God is plain to them, because God has shown it to them. **20** For his invisible attributes, namely, his eternal power and divine nature, have been clearly perceived, ever since the creation of the world, in the things that have been made. So they are without excuse. **21** For although they knew God, they <u>did not honor him as God or give thanks to him</u>, but they became futile in their thinking, and their foolish hearts were darkened.

C. Why are we here? Where are we going? Does it really matter? *What is the value of human life?* Let's just take that last one. If all you have is science, if that's the only tool in your toolshed, how do you determine the value of human life.

- If we asked a biologist or a chemist, they could tell us about the molecules that make up our body. Nitrogen, potassium, carbon, water.

But few are willing to be boiled down and sold for parts on eBay. Is that your value?
- If we asked an economist, they could help us determine what you produce, your net contribution to the economy. Is that your value?
- If we asked a sociologist, they could help determine your worth to the community, number of friends, that sort of thing. But is that your value?

D. All of those disciplines fall under the umbrella of science, yet almost anybody anywhere, would be quick to agree those are terrible ways of determining a person's worth. We inherently believe human value is more than chemical constituents, production value, or personal affiliations. The problem is that we increasingly, have a generation of children and twenty-somethings who <u>don't</u> know why they're valuable, and to a frightening degree, have begun to conclude they're not. What I want to highlight then, is that science can tell you what you're made of. It can never tell you what you <u>are</u>. **Repeat.**
- Here's where we're at. Week 1 of our study we focused on v18. And we laid down this axiom that *every time you suppress a truth, an untruth will take its place.* If you're just jumping in this morning, that's the theme for this entire sermon series. *Every time you suppress a truth, an untruth will take its place.*
- From there, we moved to v19 & 20, and considered how materialism masks what creation conveys. Materialism you'll remember is the belief there is nothing more than matter. Molecules in motion.

The Elevation of Science
A. Most of our atheist friends believe in materialism, all that exists is matter. Many atheists also hold a corollary faith in what we call scientism, the belief that science can ultimately answer any and all questions – both about the natural world and the human condition.
- The word "science" is not used in v21, but this is exactly the kind of thing v21 is highlighting. "For although they knew God, they did not honor him as God or give thanks to <u>him</u>." See whenever you suppress a truth – in this case our responsibility to honor God's authority – whenever you suppress a truth an untruth has to take its place.

- If God's authority is suppressed, something will fill that hole. Here's Alain de Botton, he's kind of second generation New Atheist. **TED Video:** Alain de Botton

B. "Of course God doesn't exist" - that's the assumption. But our atheist friends aren't stupid. They recognize, just like you and me, this world is a very hurting and broken place. So how do we fix it? If not God, then what? Well what you find is that a huge amount of the "then what" falls to scientific enterprise.

- Philosopher Wilfrid Sellars expressed, *"Science is the measure of all things."*
- Philosopher Bertrand Russell predicts, *"What science cannot discover, mankind cannot know."*
- Richard Dawkins claims, *"Scientists [are] the specialists in discovering what is true about the world and the universe."*
- Harry Kroto, a Nobel Prize-winning chemist says, *"Science is the only philosophical construct we have to determine truth with any degree of reliability."*
- And leading chemist Peter Atkins believes, *"Humanity should be proud that it has actually stumbled into [science] and that it really can attack every problem that concerns humanity with the prospect of an outcome."*

C. Very, very high view of science. You could argue its almost – idolatry. Remember, I'm not teaching this series just so you can have better conversations with the 3.1% of Americans who self-label as atheists, or the 4.6% who self-label as agnostic. It's because these presuppositions are increasingly the default view in a post-Christian society. For atheists – and millions of others too.

- For many – materialism, scientism – these views are subconscious and in the background. Philosopher Thomas Nagel is intellectually-honest enough to state out loud the motive behind scientism.

"I want atheism to be true and am made uneasy by the fact that some of the most intelligent and well-informed people I know are religious believers. It isn't just that I don't believe in God and, naturally assume I'm right in my belief. It's that I <u>hope</u> there is no God! I don't <u>want</u> there to be a God; I don't <u>want</u> the universe to be like that."

- Here's the thing. Science is awesome. It is a very useful tool. It's probably the best tool humanity ever invented, but like every other tool it works well in some places, not so well in others. And I want you to walk out of this sanctuary knowing that science can tell you what you're made of, it can never tell you what you <u>are</u>. Child of the king, purchased by the work of Christ, precious to the God of creation. That's why you, and your kids, and your aging parents, and even our enemies have inherent worth. We're image-bearers of God.
- Let me give you just two frameworks that show how the scientific endeavor, rather than being a Savior to the world – rightly used science actually points us <u>to</u> the savior of the world.

The Opportunity of Science

A. These are kind of famous, classical formulations. Number 1, the teleological argument. Have you heard that term? Also known as the fine-tuning argument. This is the truth that all the regularities and constants of physics had to be incredibly accurate to sustain the possibility of existence.

- Force of Gravity, strong nuclear force, weak nuclear force, electromagnetic force, ratio of the mass of the proton and electron – all these fall within what scientists call the goldilocks dilemma. Tiniest of windows where it can all work. Stephen Hawking for instance, maybe the most famous atheist, estimates if the expansion rate of the universe was different by one part in a hundred thousand million million, one second after the big bang, the universe would have either collapsed back on itself or could never develop in the first place.
- This is the *Carl in the hotel room* illustration, right? Is it reasonable to assume all these things perfectly organized by chance, or is it reasonable to infer design?

B. That's the teleological argument. Fine-tuning. Argument from design. The other one is called the cosmological argument. Where did the universe come from, why is there something when there ought to be nothing? If all matter, all motion, all <u>things</u> came when the big bang exploded, what made nothing explode? Here's biologist Rupert Sheldrake. **TED Video:** Rupert Sheldrake

- For me, that was the money quote. *"Give us one free miracle and we'll explain the rest."*
- In their excellent book *I Don't Have Enough Faith To Be An Atheist* (which is in our resource center), the authors write:

"[If] The Big Bang was the beginning point for the entire physical universe, time, space, and matter came into existence at that point. There was no natural world or natural law prior to the Big Bang. Since a cause cannot come after its effect, natural forces cannot account for the Big Bang. Therefore, there must be something outside of what's natural to do the job. That's exactly what the word super-natural means."

- Folks, science is a fantastic tool for studying what is natural, repeatable, observable. Science can tell you what you're made of, it can never tell you what you are. Formulations like the teleological argument and the cosmological argument show how science is meant to point us to the one with answers.

The End of Science

A. And that's the whole point of Romans 1. It says in v19, "what can be known about God is plain … [yet] they did not honor him as God or give thanks to him, but they became futile in their thinking."

- Church, I want you to remember something. Truth is true whether it has majority agreement or not. In a Wikipedia world, many of us have begun to assume truth is decided by plurality. It's not.
- If no one on the planet believed what God says, it would not change truth one iota. "All these things my hand has made (Isaiah 66), and so all these things came to be, declares the Lord."

B. As we move to a conclusion, I wanna shift the discussion a bit. After three weeks of this stuff, one of the dangers for a Sunday morning series on unbelief and atheism is that hundreds of us here, at MCC, may get the impression this isn't about us. *"I'm not an atheist, I guess Trav is preaching this so we can fix people who are."* Eh, not exactly.

- I want to introduce a term here, at the back-end of our sermon, we'll unpack more in weeks 4, 5, and 6: *functional atheism.* Or you can also call it practical atheism. Here's what it means.
- The majority at MCC confess belief in a personal God. The vast majority of Americans admit belief in some kind of God. But can I ask you – in practice, in the day to day – do your life choices show that?
- Official atheism denies God; **functional** atheism is guilty of maybe an even more astounding sin. It ignores the God it confesses.

C. I hope – I don't know if you do, but I hope – most Sundays you process with your family the sermon. Car ride home, muffin house, wherever: was the sermon helpful today? Was it true? How can it be applied?

- What I'd love for you to discuss at the chili cook-off today, or around the lunch table, or at dinner tonight, is this… do I, do we family, live in the light of the God who is there? Does that show up in our priorities? In our sacrifices?
- You may not suppress God's authority in favor of science. Scientism. That might not be <u>your</u> thing. But is there something else? Is the authority of God evident:
  1. In the way you serve your spouse?
  2. In the way you steward your finances?
  3. The things you do when no one else is looking?

D. Listen, the great enemy to Christianity is not scientism. Or materialism. Or atheism. The great enemy of Christianity is the believer's <u>unbelief</u>. Nicolai Bordyaev, a Russian philosopher, said:

"We find the most terrible form of atheism, not in the militant and passionate struggle against the idea of God himself, but in the practical atheism of everyday living in indifference and torpor. We often encounter these forms of atheism among those who are formally Christians."

- Church, you and I have a great God. Slow to anger, quick to forgive, abounding in grace. And through Christ, we have been given … life! So understand, science can tell us what we're made of. It can never tell us <u>what</u> we are. I invite you, to call upon the one who can. Let's pray…

> **The Big Idea:** Unmoored morality is morally meaningless

The Hook

A. So obviously Pastor Carl has returned from his National Lampoon's European Vacation. And you know, I thought it would be nice have Carl around again, right up until he <u>was</u> around again. I walked into our office kitchen across the street, it was like someone had thrown several gallons of paint into the room followed by a hand grenade. Paint everywhere. *"Carl!"* I said, *"What happened?"*

- *"Oh, hi Trav. Good to see you. I was trying to fix the refrigerator,"* he said – dabbing orange paint off his earlobe.

- *"The refrigerator?!"* I replied, dodging a dollop of green paint dripping off the ceiling. *"Our fridge is broken, so you threw paint around the kitchen?"*

- *"Well, it's like this,"* Carl replied. *"First day after vacation, I came in early, only to discover the fridge wasn't working, or the microwave, or the oven."*

- *"Or the coffee maker?"* I asked, sensing a pattern.

- *"Exactly!"* Carl replied. *"So I wondered, 'why's all this stuff around me broken?' And then I realized, every appliance in this kitchen is a different color … So they don't work together. I grabbed some brushes and painted them all white."*

B. *"You thought paint would make them all <u>right</u>?"* I asked.

- *"No no,"* Carl replied, *"I said all <u>white</u>. Don't be a smart aleck. But actually, the white did not make them right. The appliances were still broken. So I pulled out a can of purple paint."*

- *"Yikes – why purple,"* I asked.

- *"Seemed like a good color for the kitchen. You know purple's the color of healing, Trav. But that didn't work either. So then I tried painting all the appliances burnt orange and then forest green. Nothing's working. Trav, I feel so, as they taught me in France, les incompetent."*

- *"Tell me,"* I finally asked. *"The appliances - did you consider checking the breaker."*

- *"The breaker box!"* Carl replied with excitement. *"That's brilliant! You grab the brushes. I'll bring the paint. Pink should look fantastic."*

The Hook

A. What's true in appliance repair, is true in life. When you see something's broke, but invent your own solution, you'll probably do more harm then good.

- Remember medieval medicine – how physicians used to bleed their patients? And surgeons would chip out pieces of the skull so bad spirits could fly away. It's not just broken appliances and sick people. This is especially true in morality and ethics. When we lack wisdom, we make foolish decisions.

- That's what our text points to this morning. If you have your Bibles, please open up to the New Testament book of Romans, chapter 1. My name is Travis Bond, I serve as Senior pastor here. And we're now in week 4 of our 6 week series titled, *"The God Who is There: A Study on Belief and Unbelief."*

- If you're a brand new guest, this series is an a-typical style of preaching for us. It's a bit more academic or seminar-ish than usual. I'll explain why in a minute. For now, lets get right to the text. Romans 1. I'm gonna read seven verses this morning, but our focus will be verse 22. Romans 1, beginning at verse 16, hear now the very Word of the Lord:

16 I am <u>not</u> ashamed of the gospel, for it is the power of God for salvation to everyone who believes, to the Jew first and also to the Greek. **17** For in it the righteousness of God is revealed from faith for faith, as it is written, "The righteous shall live <u>by</u> faith." **18** For the wrath of God is revealed from heaven against all ungodliness and unrighteousness of men, who by their unrighteousness suppress the truth. **19** For what can be known about God is plain to them, because God has shown it to them. **20** For his invisible attributes, namely, his eternal power and divine nature, have been clearly perceived, ever since the creation of the world, in the things that have been made. So they are without excuse. **21** For although they knew God, they did not honor him as God or give thanks to him, but they became futile in their thinking, and their foolish hearts were darkened. **22** Claiming to be wise, they became <u>fools</u>.

Introduction

A. Would you raise your hand if you have ever unfriended someone on Facebook because they said something offensive about politics or religion or childcare or food. And how many of you know at least one person you avoid because you just don't want to talk to them.

- Used to be, in order to have a polite conversation we only had to follow the advice of Henry Higgins in *My Fair Lady* – stick to the weather and your health. But today with climate change and anti-vaxxing, not even weather and health are safe. Celeste Headlee, a host on NPR, says we live in a world in which every conversation has the potential to devolve into argument. Even the most trivial issues have someone fighting passionately for and against.

- This means conversational competence might be the most overlooked life-skill today. Your teacher told you in 4th grade: when your mouth is open you're not learning. But church, Christians ought to be setting the standard when it comes to listening well so we can graciously dialogue with both conviction and humility. And that's why we're studying for six weeks what we're studying.

B. If you've been with us for weeks 1, 2, and 3 of this series, you get what we're doing now, right? We're attempting to build, brick by brick, a fair, accurate representation of the atheistic worldview and honestly asking, is it cohesive. Is the belief in no personal God and no intelligent design the best, the most reasonable worldview we have? Or does the Bible offer something better?

- Week 1, drawn from v18, we laid down our thesis for the entire series: *"Every time you suppress a truth, an untruth takes its place."* That's the theme we keep coming back to.

- Week 2 we started fleshing that out. We considered how when you suppress <u>creation</u>, materialism takes its place. Matter is all there is. Reality is nothing more than molecules in action. No soul, no spirit, nothing beyond the grave.

- Week 3 we considered how when you suppress God's <u>authority</u>, scientism takes its place. Ultimate hope falls to science to answer questions about reality and the human condition.

- This morning, in week 4, we're looking at morality. Verse 22 says when you suppress God's wisdom – including right and wrong – when you suppress God's moral definitions, foolishness will take its place. That comes in the form of redefined, unmoored morality. And what I want you to know this morning is that *unmoored morality is morally meaningless*. **Repeat.**

Morality for Atheists

A. This may save you an argument some day – most atheists will be deeply offended if you tell them they lack a moral center. And in fact it is true, most atheists are not moral relativists. Many believe in objective good and objective evil. Child abuse, Isis, they're as disgusted as we are. The question is not do atheists believe in moral truth, it's how do they determine moral truth. That's the rub. In a worldview where no God exists, moral truth has to be determined in one of three ways.

1. Morality is determined by feeling. Christopher Hitchens, brilliant New Atheist says, *"the awareness of the difference between right and wrong is innate in human beings."* Really? I mean, in this country we tend to agree on some things like murder and pedophilia. But is that true of everything, across cultures, and across the centuries.

2. How do we determine moral truth – good and evil? Option 2, some atheists will say morality is determined by Darwinian natural selection. Whatever propagates the species is good. This is basically might makes right. And honestly, if you don't see serious problems with that one, let's grab coffee this week. Even Dawkins agrees, *"I've always said I am a passionate anti-Darwinian when it comes to the way we should organize our lives and our morality … we want to avoid basing our society on Darwinian principles."*

3. So if there's no God, how do we ground moral truth? Innate feelings? Darwinian natural selection? Third option: Morality is determined by measuring whatever maximizes human happiness. Whatever increases happiness and minimizes suffering is objectively good. Here's Sam Harris, the New Atheist who's probably done the most work in this area. **Video: Sam Harris**

B. Good looking guy. Articulate guy. But did you catch the redefinition? Values and morality now means the well-being of conscious creatures. And that, Medway Community Church, is where many of our unbelieving friends hang their hat. Not just atheists. Harris goes on to argue whatever makes people happy, whatever minimizes suffering, is morally good. Can you see the problem? The question isn't *can someone be good without God*. The question is *without God what do we mean by good*. Remember Humpty Dumpty's chat with Alice?

> *"There's glory for you!"* said Humpty Dumpty.
> *"I don't know what you mean by 'glory',"* Alice said.
> Humpty Dumpty smiled contemptuously. *'"Of course you don't — till I tell you. I meant "there's a nice knock-down argument for you!"*
> *"But 'glory' doesn't mean "a nice knock-down argument",'* Alice objected.
> *'When I use a word,'* Humpty Dumpty said, in rather a scornful tone, *'it means just what I choose it to mean — neither more nor less.'*
> *'The question is,'* said Alice, *'whether you can make words mean so many different things.'*

- See Alice got it; you can't just redefine words on a whim. Yet today good and evil is redefined so often it makes your head spin. Because it's not grounded in anything. Since when does morality get transformed into maximizing happiness. Why not maximize instead knowledge, or human reproduction, or stamp collecting.
- Here's the problem with good = more happiness; there's this nagging reality that often happiness for one often does not always happiness for the other. The clearest example is pregnancy termination. Listen to Christopher Hitchens try to work out this new definition of morality where it concerns the pre-born. He begins – please notice – by admitting outright a fetus is a living child. Quote:

> *"The words "unborn child," even when used in a politicized manner, describe a material reality. However, this only opens the argument rather than closes it. There may be many circumstances in which it is not desirable to carry a fetus to full term...it is probably less miserable an outcome than the vast number of deformed or idiot children who would otherwise have been born, or stillborn, or whose brief lives would have been a torment to themselves and others..."*

C. Pardon me while I vomit behind the organ. Can you see in this quote, the worldview that surrounds us? It's articulated loudest by New Atheism, but this principle if everywhere. Rampant individualism. Goodness and truth = whatever maximizes my happiness.

- Are you beginning to make the connection between materialism, which leads to scientism, which leads to morality redefined. Fallacies built one one on top of another. Yet unmoored morality is morally meaningless. *"I'm gonna paint these appliances a color I like, and maybe they'll start working again."* That's what it's like when we define good and evil for ourselves.

Morality for Christians

A. Later on in Romans, Paul writes this: "And we know that for those who love God all things work together for good, for those who are called according to his (do you know?) purpose."

- Have you ever noticed how <u>purpose</u> is what determines if something is used rightly? The guy who uses a lawnmower to clean his pool? We say that's incorrect. The woman who uses a canoe oar to whisk eggs? We say that's not best.

- We recognize purpose when it comes to tools and things, so what about life? Is there something you and I are supposed to *be*? Without purpose, you can't address questions of right and wrong because we have no idea what humanity is for. Anything goes.

- When your friends and your co-workers hold political, or social, or religious views that are wildly opposed to Biblical truth, this is why. It's because they hold no conviction about what they were created for. Purpose is defined by the creator. <u>Our</u> purpose is to be in right relationship with God and others. Absent that, unmoored morality is morally meaningless.

C. C.S. Lewis points out the absurdity of expecting virtue from people who are taught no virtue exists: *"In a sort of ghastly simplicity we remove the organ and demand the function. We make men without chests and expect of them virtue and enterprise. We laugh at honor and are shocked to find traitors in our midst. We castrate - then bid the eunuch 'be fruitful!'"*

Conclusion

A. There is a solution to all this — a source of goodness that's eternal. Of course, if there is an absolute measure of truth and goodness and right & wrong, it raises troubling questions — like what are the implications of falling short.

- If moral goodness is defined by me, there's a natural tendency to assume I measure up. But what if good and evil are defined by someone bigger than me?

- Well this is where the Gospel comes in. It says, you <u>don't</u> measure up. You never measured up. So God provided one who does.

- For some of us here today, that's where we need to begin. We need to stop pretending we make the rules. My friend, look to Christ!

B. But what about the rest of us. What of those who already confess faith in Jesus? It was that great theologian of the 90's, Mike Tyson, who once said, *"everybody has a plan – until they get punched in the face."*

- See every Christian in here is moral, until a broken world punches us in the face. With tragedy. With anger. Temptation. Last week I asked you to create a new category in your mind: functional atheism. It means confessing Christ but functioning day-to-day like an atheist.
- Everybody in here has two selves, can we just be honest about? We've all got the public self and the private self. This is most painfully obvious in High School, but it lasts well beyond that. One of the goals of Christianity is that over a lifetime, our two selves would gradually be more and more the exact same thing. Perfectly integrated.
- Isn't it true – the Christians you admire most are the ones who act the same in public and private. And down through the ages, those who don't act the same are the Xns who have done the most harm.

C. Functional atheism means a cracked, fragmented life. So God's definitions for right and wrong, we live that on Sunday. Morning. For an hour. But it doesn't transform my marriage. Or my politics. Or my college choice. God's definition of right and wrong doesn't impact my views on *sexual ethics*, or *social media*, or *Game of Thrones*, or *work ethic*.

- Functional atheism means I will define as good that which maximizes my happiness and minimizes my displeasure. I'm just gonna keep painting these appliances the color I like – until they start working.

C. But friends, Christ has come. And he has said child, I know what is good and noble and pure and just. John 10:10, "The thief comes only to steal and kill and destroy. I came that you may have life and have it (what's it say?) abundantly."

- This table is not for perfectly moral people. It's for messy people willing to confess, *"I have tried to invent my own morality." I have lived as if 'good' means 'what suits me.'"* This table is for those who see how we have hurt others because we're selfish. So we're prepared to confess that sin and know in Christ, there is grace. There is <u>so</u> <u>much</u> <u>grace</u>. Will our deacons please come forward...

> **The Big Idea:** For life to have true meaning, upon God we must be leaning.

The Hook

A. So the other day, Carl says to me, *"Trav – we should go rafting together."* "Rafting Carl? I dunno it's kind of a busy week here…" *"Nope, Trav – we need to get outside, enjoy this beautiful, cloud-drenched New England weather. Let's go."*

- So, we packed up our gear – all that … rafting gear…Carl and I have – and we we hit the open river.
- For hours we enjoyed ourselves on the water until, suddenly, we heard a quiet roar. Squinting into the distance, I noticed a rather disturbing, absence-of-horizon look. *"Carl! Waterfall!!"*
- Frantically we spun the raft around and began trying to paddle to one bank of the river, then the other, but the current was too strong. Kept pulling us back into the center.

B. Finally, we realized by paddling with all our might straight upstream we could almost hold the raft in place, but still couldn't make any progress away from the falls. And then, after a while, over my shoulder I saw him. Carl, with his hands relaxed behind his head, laying on his back.

- *"Carl, I need your help here!   This is no time for a nap."*
- *"Oh Trav,"* Carl said as he tossed his paddle into the river and stretched out again with a smile. *"I say we just enjoy our last ride."* **Waterfall picture.**

C. Folks, if atheism is true we are all the guys in the raft. What awaits us, our civilization, our planet, our universe – is extinction, no matter what we do. So lean back, enjoy the ride, but let's be honest about what's ahead.

- My name is Travis Bond, I serve as Senior Pastor here, and this morning is week 5 of a 6 week series we're calling "The God Who is There" a study on belief and unbelief.
- If you have your Bibles, please open up to our anchor passage in the New Testament book of Romans, chapter 1. Written by the apostle Paul, this passage is an autopsy on truth suppression. Or unbelief. Romans 1 lays out the consequences of suppressing the knowledge of God.

- I'm gonna read 8 verses this morning, but our focus will be on verse 23. Romans 1, beginning at verse 16, hear now the very Word of the Lord:

16 I am <u>not</u> ashamed of the gospel, for it is the power of God for salvation to everyone who believes, to the Jew first and also to the Greek. **17** For in it the righteousness of God is revealed from faith for faith, as it is written, "The righteous shall live <u>by</u> faith." **18** For the wrath of God is revealed from heaven against all ungodliness and unrighteousness of men, who by their unrighteousness suppress the truth. **19** For what can be known about God is plain to them, because God has shown it to them. **20** For his invisible attributes, namely, his eternal power and divine nature, have been clearly perceived, ever since the creation of the world, in the things that have been made. So they are without excuse. **21** For although they knew God, they did not honor him as God or give thanks to him, but they became futile in their thinking, and their foolish hearts were darkened. **22** Claiming to be wise, they became <u>fools</u>, **23** and exchanged the glory of the immortal God for images resembling mortal man and birds and animals and creeping things.

Introduction

A. In the Old Testament, if you read Deuteronomy 6, it says we are to love God with all our heart, all our soul, and all our strength. In the New Testament, Gospel of Luke, Jesus adds something. He says, "you shall love the Lord your God with all your heart and with all your soul and with all your strength and with all your (do you know?) mind."

- See intellectually lazy Christianity is no Christianity at all. Mark Noll once said the scandal of the evangelical mind is that there is not <u>much</u> of an evangelical mind. Richard Hofstadter writes in his Pulitzer-prize winning book *Anti-Intellectualism in American Life*, quote, *"for many Christians, humble ignorance is a far more noble quality that a cultivated mind."*

B. Listen, to whatever extent that's true, that's bad. The church should be top percentile for thoughtful, well-reasoned conviction. And I say that for two reasons:

1. Romans 12 commands us to "be transformed by the renewing of your (what?) mind." That's not an option. It's a command, because what we believe about God is the baseline thing about us. Everyone inevitably moves toward their mental understanding of God.

2. The second reason our mind matters is because we're taught in 2 Corinthians 10 that "we demolish arguments and every pretension that sets itself up <u>against</u> the knowledge of God and we take captive <u>every thought</u> to make it obedient to Christ."

C. This is a bright church, which means there is no excuse for us to lack a robust, full-orbed understanding of why we believe what we believe. That's a lot of what these six weeks are about. We're seeking brick by brick to build a fair, true representation of an atheist's or an agnostic's or an unbeliever's worldview then honestly asking, is that cohesive? Is that convincing? Or does Scripture offer something better? If you're jumping in for the first time today, here's where we've been. Our overarching thesis, derived from Romans 1 verse 18, is this: *Every time you suppress a truth, an untruth take its place.* So we ask Romans 1 what are the suppressions at work around us?

- Verses 19-20, suppress God's creation, MATERIALISM takes its place.
- Verse 21, suppress God's authority, today SCIENTISM takes its place.
- Verse 22, suppress God's morality, FOOLISHNESS takes it place.
- Which brings us to this morning. Verse 23. We suppress God's glory. When you have no God, when you have no creator, what do you have? Here's Christopher Hitchens, one of the four most well-known New Atheists, answering the question, "What is the purpose of life?"

Meaning for Atheists

A. Now here's the thing, I didn't edit out the real answer. That was from a debate a couple years before Hitchens was diagnosed with cancer, and that really is the answer he likes to give to this question. Obviously being funny. Tongue planted firmly in cheek. I get it. And yet — nothing else offered afterwards. The implication, there is no grand purpose to life. It's a silly question.

- Understand — this concept of ultimate meaning, and purpose, it often makes atheists uncomfortable. Listen to the poetic gloom of Bertrand Russell, a 20th century New Atheist before New Atheism was a thing:

"Man is the product of causes which had no pre-vision of the end they were achieving; his origin, his growth, his hopes and fears, his loves and his beliefs, are but the outcome of accidental collocations of atoms; no fire, no heroism, no intensity of thought and feeling, can preserve an individual life beyond the grave; all the labors of the ages, all the devotion, all the

inspiration, all the noonday brightness of human genius, are destined to extinction in the vast death of the solar system, and the whole temple of Man's achievement must inevitably be buried beneath the debris of a universe in ruins ... Only within the scaffolding of these truths, only on the firm foundation of unyielding despair, can the soul's habitation henceforth be safely built."

- Sounds like a fun guy at a party, huh? I disagree but at least Russell's honest about his worldview. If there is no God, we're all just a guy in a raft, heading for the falls. "Claiming to be wise, (it says in verse 22) they became <u>fools</u>, and exchanged the glory of the immortal God."

B. Atheist cosmologist Lawrence Krauss memorably said, *"We are a 1% bit of pollution within the universe. We are completely insignificant."* Atheist philosopher John Gray adds, *"We cannot escape the finality of tragedy...there is no redemption from being human."* And Christian author Andy Bannister sums up the situation: *"If there is no God...you're alone in a universe that cares as little about you (and your enjoyment) as it does about the fate of the amoeba, the ant, or the aardvark. There's no hope, there's no justice, and there's nothing inherently wrong with poverty – so quit protesting."*

- Now as you might guess, these perspectives are a pretty tough sell to the general population so here's New Atheist Dan Dannett, a philosophy professor right here at Tufts, making a heroic attempt to develop meaning out of meaninglessness.

C. So there you go. You weren't designed by a creator. You have no inherent significance. So you invent your own meaning. You make your own morality. This is the prevailing view of our day. Consciously for a few. Unconsciously for many. But even in the last month, be it Target bathroom absurdities, or painful presidential primaries, our cultural hens are coming home to roost. There's no God, there's no meaning, there's no morality. We just make it up as we go along.

Meaning for Christians

A. And so can you guess – why is it we have an entire generation of millennials experiencing despair at epidemic proportions, many reaching the conclusion life might not be worth living at all? Why is it millions in Gen X have reached their late 30's and early 40's yet feel profound emptiness having <u>achieved</u> career, financial, and family goals.

- Victor Frankle was, a Jewish psychologist, who suffered incredibly in the concentration camps of World War II, but that's not the tragedy Frankl writes about. Quote:

"For too long we have been dreaming a dream from which we are now waking up: the dream that if we just improve the socioeconomic situation of people everything will be okay, people will become happy. The truth is that as the struggle for survival has subsided, the question has emerged: survival for what? Ever more people today have the means to live, but no meaning to live for."

B. Speaking from the perspective of the pastor's office, where I often witness pain and despair not everyone does, I'm tellin' you that quote is dead on. Which is why I want you to know the Bible offers a decidedly different perspective. Psalm 138, the Psalmist writes, "The Lord will fulfill His purpose for me. Your steadfast love, O Lord, endures forever."

- Or, in one of the most encouraging texts in all of Scripture, you know this one, right? Jeremiah 29. Let's say it together: "For I know the plans I have for you, declares the Lord, plans to prosper you and not to harm you, plans to give you hope and a future." You see when we rest by faith in Christ, our purpose, our cross-shaped purpose becomes the glory of God and the good of his people.

C. Someone in the back holds up their hand. *"Uh Trav, all the God and Jesus talk may sound lovely, but it doesn't make it real."* I agree. Wishful thinking does not make our Bible real. If we live in a godless, materialistic, universe no Jesus-fish hallmark sentiment about hope and heaven and ultimate meaning makes any of it true.

- Of course, the knife cuts both ways; because Dennett's claim that we can make eternal meaning and purpose out of nothing, that's not true either.

- If the universe really is meaningless, undirected, and pointless, you and I are here only because a long chain of our biological ancestors managed to reproduce successfully having been the byproduct of spontaneous combustion of life. You and I are just a guy in a raft heading for the falls.

- Yet if that's true, we are left with a puzzling mystery. What is it about human beings that make us the only creatures who ask, "why?" Bannister writes give a cow grass and the occasional bull, she's happy for life. Humans though, seem strikingly dissatisfied with only material things. Quote:

"What could it have been that possessed evolution, normally so thrifty with its juggling of genes, to equip us and us alone among the animal kingdom with desires for ... value, meaning, purpose, and significance."

Conclusion

A. Here's where we finish. The Christian author Tolkien, *Lord of the Rings*, he once penned a short story about a struggling painter named Niggle who spent his entire life trying to create a beautiful painting of a forest vista with mountains in the distance. But Niggle was so desperate to make the picture perfect he never finished more than a single leaf on a single tree. Endlessly obsessing, he eventually fell ill and died without completing his work. But as Tolkien tells the story, it was after his death, when Niggle arrived in heaven, he approached the edge of the heavenly country and he saw a tree. In fact, it was *his* tree – finished and complete – every leaf made perfect.

- Christianity teaches all people can experience that kind of fulfillment, you see in the Niggle metaphor. When we're caught up into God's purposes, our lives are no longer meaningless but woven together into God's redemptive design.

B. Which means this time tomorrow, your work in the office...

- Or that crying baby your awake with all night tonight...
- Or all the tears your shedding to save a marriage on life support...
- That person you talk to at jury duty. That homeless mom you welcome into your family. Those are tiny little half-finished leaves on canvas, that God gathers up and makes perfect. Let's pray...

The Big Idea: Do you really believe, that what you believe, is really real?

The Hook

A. *"Bon Appetit!"* said the waiter, as he set our lunch before us. I looked at my food, I suppose, with something less than enthusiasm.

- *"Anything wrong?"* Carl asked.
- *"Nothing a little meat wouldn't solve,"* I replied.
- *"Hey,"* Carl said, *"I'm really grateful you were willing to do lunch at this place. Ever since we got back from Europe, Jean and I have been very strict vegans."* I mumbled "no problem" as I tentatively poked my black bean veggie patty. Personally, I prefer food that was once healthy and running around in the fresh air.

B. Suddenly sitting at our table, as I looked up at him, Carl produced a small Tupperware from his pants pocket, furtively glance around, then shook its contents over his salad. He caught my eye watching him and simply mouthed, *"Tuna."*

- *"Tuna?!"* I said, eying the seafood joint right across the street.
- *"Shh"* Carl replied. *"Not all vegans appreciate my liberal approach. You see, I'm a vegan, but I eat fish. Fish doesn't count as a meat because it lives in the water."*
- *"Let me get this straight, Carl. You tell folks you're a vegan, but you still eat fish."*
- *"Correct,"* Carl said. *"And Calamari. I have a fisherman friend I trade with."*
- *"So would that be ... squid pro quo?"* I asked.
- *"Haha. Very funny, Trav. Also I still eat, crab, shellfish, and lobster."*
- *"Carl, you're the strangest vegan I ever met."*

C. *"Duck too,"* Carl replied. *"Ducks live <u>on</u> the water, right?"* He paused for a moment. *"And cows. I eat cows because they live <u>near</u> the water."*

- *"Wh...Wait a sec. So you're telling me you claim to Jean, and your friends, and your colleagues that you're a strict vegan, but the whole time any animal that lives in, on, or within sight of water is <u>fair game</u>?"*
- *"Right,"* Carl replied as he produced another Tupperware. *"Speaking of 'fair game', would you like to try my venison jerky."*

D. This whole pick and choose approach sounds pretty silly in the context of diet. But I wonder, how many of us here today embrace a view of the Christian life that looks kinda like Carl's approach to veganism. I'm a Christian, buuuut I like to do this. I put my faith in Jesus, buuuut I also put my faith in this.

- If you have your Bibles, would you please open up, for our last time, to the book of Romans, chapter 1. If you want to use one of the Black Bibles, this is page 939.
- For six weeks our anchor passage has been these ten verses. I'm gonna read starting at v16, although our focus will be the end, verses 24 and 25. Romans 1, verse 16, hear now the very Word of the Lord:

16 I am <u>not</u> ashamed of the gospel, for it is the power of God for salvation to everyone who believes, to the Jew first and also to the Greek. **17** For in it the righteousness of God is revealed from faith for faith, as it is written, "The righteous shall live <u>by</u> faith." **18** For the wrath of God is revealed from heaven against all ungodliness and unrighteousness of men, who by their unrighteousness suppress the truth. **19** For what can be known about God is plain to them, because God has shown it to them. **20** For his invisible attributes, namely, his eternal power and divine nature, have been clearly perceived, ever since the creation of the world, in the things that have been made. So they are without excuse. **21** For although they knew God, they did not honor him as God or give thanks to him, but they became futile in their thinking, and their foolish hearts were darkened. **22** Claiming to be wise, they became <u>fools</u>, **23** and exchanged the glory of the immortal God for images resembling mortal man and birds and animals and creeping things. **24** Therefore God gave them up in the lusts of their hearts to impurity, to the dishonoring of their bodies among themselves, **25** because they exchanged the truth about God for a lie and worshiped and served the creature rather than the Creator, who is blessed forever! Amen.

Introduction
A. If you're a brand new guest this morning you'll be helped to know we're finishing today a series called *The God Who is There*. For the past five sermons in this six sermon series, we've been attempting to honestly, and respectfully build an understanding of our atheistic friend's, or the agnostics, or the unbeliever's worldview. What do many of our non-Christian friends believe, and why?

- We're trying to be honest about that and then honestly say, OK, is that cohesive? Is a Godless reality the best explanation for the world around us or does Scripture offer something better?

B. Our theme from Romans 1 is this: *Every time you suppress a truth an untruth takes its place.* This has been what we keep coming back to: *Every time you suppress a truth an untruth takes its place.* From there, we've just followed the path laid out in Romans 1.

- Verses 19-20, suppress God's creation, MATERIALISM takes its place.
- Verse 21, suppress God's authority, today SCIENTISM takes its place.
- Verse 22, suppress God's morality, FOOLISHNESS takes its place.
- From last week Verse 23, suppress God's glory, MEANINGLESSNESS takes its place. That was five weeks.

C. This morning, is a bit different. Last two verses of our passage in a way circle us back to where we started. But now I wanna pivot. This morning I don't wanna talk as much about other beliefs. We've done that. This morning, I wanna talk about our beliefs. I want to take an honest look at ourselves. Because verse 24 & 25 say this: *suppress God's truth* (or you might say suppress God's existence) *idolatry takes its place.* **Repeat.**

Idolatry for Atheists

1. I'm gonna borrow a question from a professor named Del Tackett, and I want you to roll this around in your head a little bit. Do you really believe that what you believe is really real?

- Many of you will know the account in Exodus 3 and 4 of a man named Moses coming upon a burning bush. It says God spoke out of the bush. And God asked Moses to do some pretty hard stuff. And in that moment, Moses had to decide something.
- Do I really believe that what I believe is really real? It's the same question God's people have had to ask ever since. Do I have reason to believe God is there. If so – will I trust him?

2. After service a few weeks ago, someone mentioned a great word picture: If walking down the street you come upon 1,000 nickels on the sidewalk, every one of them heads up in nice, neat rows, what inference will you immediately make? Somebody did this. This screams design.

- Most people in this room – this is church after all – most people in this room look at the world around us and says, somebody did this. This universe screams design. And so we call ourselves – vegans. I mean, Christians.

- But like our imaginary vegan, our beliefs and our actions are often inconsistent. Verse 25: "They exchanged the truth about God for a lie and worshipped and served the creature." Some of us claim we're Christians, yet make decisions as if we're atheists. As if God is not directing or impacting or guiding our life. And we turn, a la verse 25, to idols. Listen to Tim Keller explain modern day idolatry.

B. Are you savvy enough to perceive the idols in your life? Emma Goldman was an anarchist and an atheist born in 1869. And she wrote that God, *"has dominated humanity and will continue to do so until man will raise his head to the sunlit day … How far man will be able to find his relation to his fellows will depend entirely upon how much he can outgrow his dependence upon God."* The theological problem with that is that whenever you suppress God – be it his truth, his existence, our dependence upon him – idolatry takes God's place.

- Whenever you suppress a truth, an untruth takes its place. Whenever you suppress God's truth, idolatry takes its place. Because you and I were created to be worshippers. We will always find something to worship.
- It's not just the unbeliever who makes little idols. It's believers too. It's any Christian who begins to move their trust and dependence off of God onto something else. And so I wanna ask you this morning, after 5 or 6 weeks talking about worldviews and atheism and belief and unbelief: do you really believe that what you believe is really real? Or, are you both an educated Christian and a functional atheist. Professing God but living without him.
- Christian Author Richard Lovelace once wrote:

"Those who are not secure in Christ cast about for spiritual life preservers with which to support their confidence, and in their frantic search they cling not only to the shreds of ability and righteousness they find in themselves, but they fix upon their race, their membership in a party, their familiar social and ecclesiastical patterns, and their culture as means of self-recommendation."

C. In other words, we will make an idol out of anything. Even good things. Idolatry is often simply making good things ultimate things. That's what verse 25 is talking about. "Exchanging the truth about God for a lie [they] worshiped and served the creature rather than the creator."

Idolatry for Functional Atheists

A. It's been 50 years and a month since the famous Time Magazine Cover *Is God Dead?* 5o years ago, 97% of Americans who were polled believed in God. Today, it's still 93%. 63% of Americans are absolutely certain of the existence of God. Another 20% are fairly certain. But here's the thing: when it comes to the church, our concern has never been percentages. Rather, it's how how many of us are <u>walking</u> with God?

- The American church is facing significant cultural challenges today. From outside. That is true, but understand, nothing does as much harm to Christian witness as when half the Christians don't even act like half Christians even half of the time. Do you really believe that what you believe is really real? If so, does it impact the things you watch, the things you fantasize about, the way you spend your time, the way you spend your money, and the words that come from your mouth. Or, like our imaginary vegan, do you pick and choose what parts of your conviction you wanna follow? Have you set up false idols on your own mantle, right beside the cross?
- Sometimes their hard to spot. The idols in our life. It's probably a whole sermon series, but let me give you four quick diagnostics you can use to help answer the question, do I really believe that what I believe is really real?
  1. *Understand, a man's true religion is what he does in his solitude.* How do you spend your time when no one is watching.
  2. *Your checkbook reveals what your speech conceals.* Where do you spend your money? Why do you spend your money? Who do you spend it on? Does God get first fruits or leftovers? You show me your checkbook, I'll show you your priorities.
  3. *How do you response to unanswered prayers or frustrated goals.* Do you act like God is sovereign when things go off the rails? Or do you get snippy with your spouse, harsh with your kids, and complain as if God is absent.
  4. *Fill in the blank, I would be happy if only _____.* Whatever's in that blank right now, is probably what you worship.

B. I've got a favor to ask. A couple months back, I sent out a survey. You guys were great. You filled it out. Shared it on FB. I got hundreds of responses. Hugely helpful to me preparing this series. I wanna do it one more time. But don't share it. It's just for folks who heard any of these sermons. I'll blast it out on Wednesday. A lot of it's the same questions as before. That's intentional. And then a few different questions as well. I would very much appreciate it you took the time.

- Because you know, after six weeks, I hope we understand this much: Believing like an atheist is kinda hard. Acting like an atheist, is far too easy. Functional atheism just kinda creeps into life. So what can we do? Two things:
- #1, Roll back on Christ. Today, get alone with God and confess, *"Lord, I think I often live as if you're not there. I know you are. I believe. Help my unbelief."* That's #1.

C. #2, Open up your hand. This is where we'll finish. Moses at that burning bush. Remember what God asked him? He had Moses take off his shoes, holy ground. Told him to go to Pharoah. Do hard stuff. Moses got scared, pushed back. And God asked him a question (beginning of Exodus 4): *"What's in your hand?"* And of course it was a shepherd's staff. And God said, *"throw it down."* And God turned it into a snake. And then God turned it back into a staff. And if you're reading all this for the first time you're like, *"What is that about."* Rick Warren, he says God never does a miracle just to show off. There's always something around it. A shepherd's staff represented three things. Stay with me here:

1. For Moses, it represented his identity. He was a shepherd. That's what he did. All day, that's who he was.
2. # 2, a shepherd's staff represented income. All his assets were tied up in sheep. In those days nobody had bank accounts or stock options. Wealth is wrapped up in flocks.
3. So it represented his identity. It represented his income. #3, it represented his influence. This is how you move sheep. By hook or by crook. You pull 'em or you poke 'em.

D. Listen, God never asks a question he doesn't know the answer to. When God asks a question it's for your benefit not his. So where did he start with Moses. He said, *"Moses, what's in your hand? That thing that represents your identity, your income, influence. Throw it down and I'll make it come alive. I will use what you possess to accomplish more than you ever dreamed."* You've seen the movies. God was always working through the staff to accomplish these amazing miracles.

- And I guess that's why I preached these six sermons. Because this church is amazingly gifted. Not just one thing. A hundred things. Intellect, wealth, talent, community influence. What's in your hand, my friend?

- What are you gonna <u>do</u> with what God has given to you. Your identity, your income, your influence. Throw it down. All these areas we're tempted to make little false idols. Good things we turn into ultimate things. Throw it down before the living God. And then you'll have your answer: Do I really believe that what I believe is really real?

APPENDIX C
Posttest Survey

Welcome!

Thank you for participating (perhaps for a second time!) in research for my doctoral studies; your time is greatly appreciated. The following survey is broken into three, brief sections with multiple choice options. The fourth and final section is composed of a few, *optional* questions that allow for open-ended response.

Total time to complete the survey will be approximately 5 to 6 minutes. All data submitted is SSL encrypted and completely anonymous. The survey can be completed using either desktop or mobile devices.

Please click the button below to begin...

Sincerely,
Travis Bond

UNDERSTANDING ATHEISM: A Research Project Survey

Section 1 of 4: Demographic Information (8 Questions)

* 1. Are you male or female?

- Male
- Female

* 2. What is your age range?

- under 18
- 18-29
- 30-39
- 40-49
- 50-64
- 65+

* 3. How do you describe your race?

○ American Indian or Alaskan Native

○ Asian

○ Black or African American

○ Latino

○ White or Caucasian

○ Some other race (please specify)

[   ]

* 4. In what area of the United States do you currently reside?

○ New England

○ Mid-Atlantic

○ South

○ South-West

○ Mid-West

○ Pacific States

○ Some other region or a different country (please specify)

[   ]

* 5. What is the highest level of education you have completed or the highest degree you have received?

○ Less than high school degree

○ High school degree or equivalent (e.g., GED)

○ Associate degree

○ Bachelor degree

○ Masters Degree

○ Doctoral Degree

* 6. Which of the following best describes your religious affiliation?

○ Agnostic

○ Atheist

○ Buddhist

○ Christian

○ Hindu

○ Jewish

○ Muslim

○ No affiliation

○ Other (please specify)

[   ]

* 7. Which of the following best describes your current job?

○ For-profit organization

○ Full-time homemaker

○ Nonprofit organization

○ Student

○ Unemployed

○ Self-Employed

○ Retired

○ Other (please specify)

[   ]

* 8. How many sermons would you estimate you heard in the recent MCC preaching series "The God Who is There?"

NO Sermons	1 sermon	2 sermons	3 sermons	4 sermons	5 sermons	6 Sermons
○	○	○	○	○	○	○

UNDERSTANDING ATHEISM: A Research Project Survey

Section 2 of 4: Social Engagement with Atheism (7 Questions)

* 9. To the best of my knowledge, I often engage in day-to-day conversation with atheists *(regarding work, marriage, parenting, politics, etc):*

strongly disagree	tend to disagree	neutral	tend to agree	strongly agree	I Don't Know
○	○	○	○	○	○

* 10. To the best of my knowledge, I often engage in spiritual conversation with atheists *(regarding eternity, personal faith, the way faith interacts with everyday issues, etc):*

strongly disagree	tend to disagree	neutral	tend to agree	strongly agree	I Don't Know
○	○	○	○	○	○

* 11. I feel well equipped to explain and defend my religious faith in conversation with an atheist:

strongly disagree	tend to disagree	neutral	tend to agree	strongly agree	I Don't Know
○	○	○	○	○	○

* 12. I believe atheism is an increasing demographic in the region where I reside:

strongly disagree	tend to disagree	neutral	tend to agree	strongly agree	I Don't Know
○	○	○	○	○	○

* 13. I believe atheism is an increasing demographic throughout the United States:

strongly disagree	tend to disagree	neutral	tend to agree	strongly agree	I Don't Know
○	○	○	○	○	○

* 14. I believe atheism is an increasing demographic worldwide:

strongly disagree	tend to disagree	neutral	tend to agree	strongly agree	I Don't Know
○	○	○	○	○	○

* 15. I believe present-day atheists are increasingly outspoken when compared to atheists 20 years ago:

strongly disagree	tend to disagree	neutral	tend to agree	strongly agree	I Don't Know
○	○	○	○	○	○

UNDERSTANDING ATHEISM: A Research Project Survey

Section 3 of 4: Personal Engagement with Atheism (9 Questions)

* 16. I have a good understanding of the atheistic world and life view(*e.g. general atheistic beliefs*):

strongly disagree	tend to disagree	neutral	tend to agree	strongly agree
○	○	○	○	○

* 17. I have a good understanding of how atheists view the basis of morality:

strongly disagree	tend to disagree	neutral	tend to agree	strongly agree
○	○	○	○	○

* 18. I have a good understanding of how atheists view the origin of the universe:

strongly disagree	tend to disagree	neutral	tend to agree	strongly agree
○	○	○	○	○

* 19. I have a good understanding of how atheists view the purpose of human life:

strongly disagree	tend to disagree	neutral	tend to agree	strongly agree
○	○	○	○	○

* 20. I have a good understanding of how atheists view the role of science:

strongly disagree	tend to disagree	neutral	tend to agree	strongly agree
○	○	○	○	○

* 21. I believe the Christian Bible offers a convincing response to an atheistic understanding of reality:

strongly disagree	tend to disagree	neutral	tend to agree	strongly agree
○	○	○	○	○

* 22. The recent MCC preaching series "The God Who is There" has left me MORE confident of the Christian faith than I was before?

strongly disagree	tend to disagree	neutral	tend to agree	strongly agree
○	○	○	○	○

* 23. The recent MCC preaching series "The God Who is There" has left me BETTER equipped to defend the Christian faith than I was before?

strongly disagree	tend to disagree	neutral	tend to agree	strongly agree
○	○	○	○	○

* 24. Regardless of my publicly stated religion, I increasingly lean toward atheism as my own personal conviction:

strongly disagree	tend to disagree	neutral	tend to agree	strongly agree
○	○	○	○	○

UNDERSTANDING ATHEISM: A Research Project Survey

Section 4 of 4: Optional Responses (3 Questions)

25. In what way(s), if any, was the recent MCC preaching series "The God Who is There?" most helpful to you?

26. In what way(s), if any, could the recent MCC preaching series "The God Who is There" have been more helpful? What constructive criticism can you offer?

27. Any additional comments, recommendations, or suggestions?

BIBLIOGRAPHY

Andrews, Seth. *Deconverted: A Journey from Religion to Reason*. Denver, Co: Outskirts Press, 2013.

Atkins, Peter. *Burning Questions* TV documentary, Episode 2: "God and Science", accessed February 16, 2016. http://www.burningquestions.ca.

Baggini, Julian. *Atheism: A Very Short Introduction*. New York: Oxford University Press, 2003.

Bannister, Andy. *The Atheist Who Didn't Exist, Or: the Dreadful Consequences of Bad Arguments*. Oxford, England: Monarch Books, 2015.

Barker, Dan. *Godless: How an Evangelical Preacher Became One of America's Leading Atheists*. Ulysses Press: Berkeley, CA, 2008.

Berger, Peter L. *A Rumor of Angels*. New York: Anchor Books, 1970.

Boyne, Ian. Why God Might Exist. March 8, 2015. Accessed on January 26, 2016. http://jamaica-gleaner.com/article/focus/20150308/ian-boyne-why-god-might-exist.

Brockman, John ed., *Intelligent Thought: Science versus the Intelligent Design Movement*. New York: Vintage, 2006.

Brooks, Rodney. *Flesh and Machines: How Robots Will Change Us*. New York: Pantheon, 2002.

Brown, Andre. "Science is the only road to truth? Don't be absurd" July 4, 2011. Accessed on January 22, 2016. http://www.theguardian.com/commentisfree /andrewbrown/2011/jul/04/harry-kroto-science-truth.

Carrier, Richard. *Sense and Goodness without God: A Defense of Metaphysical Naturalism*. Bloomington, IN: Author House, 2005.

Carter, Maureen. "What is Truth?" Accessed March 14, 2015. http://www.whatistruth.org.uk/whatistruth.php.

Craig, William Lane. *Reasonable Faith*. Wheaton, IL: Crossway, 2008.

Crick, Francis. *What Mad Pursuit: A Personal View of Scientific Discovery*. New York: Basic Books, 1988.

Dawkins, Richard. *A Devil's Chaplain: Selected Writings*, London: Phoenix Press, 2004.

_____. *The God Delusion*. Boston: Houghton Mifflin Company, 2008.

_____. *The Selfish Gene*. New York: Oxford University Press, 2006.

_____. "What Use is Religion? Part 1." Free Inquiry, June/July. Accessed June 14, 2016. http://www.beliefnet.com/news/2001/04/what-good-is-religion.aspx.

Davies, Paul. "Taking Science on Faith." November 24, 2007. Accessed January 14, 2016. http://www.nytimes.com/2007/11/24/opinion/24davies.html.

_____. "The Origin of Life II: How Did It Begin?" Accessed January 28, 2016. http://aca.mq.edu.au/PaulDavies /publications/papers/OriginsOfLife_II.pdf.

Dennett, Daniel C. *Breaking the Spell: Religion as a Natural Phenomenon*. New York: The Penguin Group, 2006.

_____ and Linda Lascola. *Caught in the Pulpit: Leaving Belief Behind*. United States of America, 2013.

_____. *Darwin's Dangerous Idea: Evolution and the Meanings of Life*. London: Simon & Schuster, 1996.

Charles Darwin. *The Autobiography of Charles Darwin 1809-1882*. ed. Nora Barlow. London: Collins, 1958.

_____. *The Life and Letters of Charles Darwin*. New York: D. Appleton and Company, 1896.

Doane, Darren. "Collision." Accessed on April 11, 2015. https://www.youtube.com /watch?v=cCUmKP4NFKs.

D'Souza, Dinesh. *What's So Great about Christianity*. Washington, DC: Regnery, 2007.

Eagleton, Terry. *Culture and the Death of God*. New Haven, CT: Yale University Press, 2014.

Feser, Edward. "Not Understanding Nothing: A Review of *A Universe from Nothing*." June 20, 2012. Accessed January 15, 2016. http://www.firstthings.com/article /2012/05 /not-understanding-nothing.

Flew, Antony. *There Is a God: How the World's Most Notorious Atheist Changed His Mind*. New York: HarperOne, 2007.

Gauchet, Marcel. *The Disenchantment of the World: A Political History of Religion*. Princeton NJ: Princeton University Press, 1997.

Geisler, Norman L. and Daniel J. McCoy. *The Atheists's Fatal Flaw: Exposing Conflicting Beliefs*. Grand Rapids, Michigan: Baker Books, 2014.

_____ and Frank Turek. *I Don't Have Enough Faith to Be an Atheist*. Wheaton, Illinois: Crossway, 2004.

Gill, Victoria. "Big Bang: Is There Room for God?" October 19, 2012. Accessed on February 16, 2016. http://www.bbc.com/news/science-environment-19997789.

Goldman, Emma. "The Philosophy of Atheism," in *The Portable Atheist: Essential Readings for the Nonbelievers*, edited by Christopher Hitchens. Philadelphia: Da Capo Press, 2007.

Gray, John. *Heresies: Against Progress and Other Illusions*. London: Granta, 2004.

_____. *The Silence of Animals*. New York: Farrar, Straus, and Giroux, 2013.

_____. *Straw Dogs*. New York: Farrar, Straus, and Giroux, 2007.

Grossman, Lisa. "Why Physicists Can't Avoid a Creation Event." January 11, 2012. Accessed on January 22, 2016. https://www.newscientist.com/article /mg21328474-400-why-physicists-cant-avoid-a-creation-event/.

Guinness, Os. *Fool's Talk: Recovering The Art of Christian Persuasion*. Downers Grove, IL: InterVarsity Press, 2015.

Harris Sam. *The End of Faith: Religion, Terror, and the Future of Reason*. New York: W.W. Norton & Company, 2004.

Harris, Sam. *Free Will*. New York: Free Press: A Division of Simon & Schuster, Inc., 2012.

_____. *Letter to a Christian Nation*. New York: Vintage Books, 2008.

_____. *The Moral Landscape: How Science Can Determine Human Values*. New York: Free Press, 2010.

_____. *Waking Up: A Guide to Spirituality Without Religion*. New York: Simon & Schuster, 2014.

Haught, John F. *God and the New Atheism: A Critical Response to Dawkins, Harris, and Hitchens*. Louisville: Westminster, 2008.

Hitchens, Christopher. *God is not Great: How Religion Poisons Everything.* New York: Hatchette Book Group, 2009.

_____. *Hitch 22: A Memoir.* New York: Hatchette Book Group, 2010.

_____. *Mortality.* New York: Hatchette Book Group, 2012.

Hitchens, Peter. *The Rage Against God: How Atheism Led Me to Faith.* Grand Rapids, MI: Zondervan, 2010.

Hughes, Austin. "The Folly of Scientism." Accessed April 17, 2015. http://www.thenewatlantis.com/publications/the-folly-of-scientism.

Huxley, Aldous. "Beliefs," in *Ends and Means: An Inquiry into the Nature of Ideals.* Piscataway, NJ: Transaction Publishers, 2012.

_____. *Ends and Means: An Inquiry into the Nature of Ideals and into the Methods Employed for their Realization.* London: Chatto and Windus, 1941.

Isaacson, Walter. *Einstein: His Life and Universe.* New York: Simon & Schuster, 2007.

James, William. *The Varieties of Religious Experience.* New York: Penguin, 1982.

Keller, Timothy and Katherine Leary Alsdorf. *Every Good Endeavor: Connecting Your Work to God's Work.* New York: Dutton, 2012.

_____. *The Reason for God.* New York: Dutton, 2008.

Kirsch, Arthur. *Auden and Christianity.* Chelsea, MI: Sheridan Books, 2005.

Krauss, Lawrence M. *A Universe From Nothing: Why There is Something Rather Than Nothing.* New York: Atria Paperbacks, 2012.

Lewis, C.S. *The Abolition of Man.* New York: MacMillan, 1947.

_____. *Miracles*. New York: HarperCollins, 1974.

_____. *The Problem of Pain*. New York: Macmillan, 1944.

_____. *The Weight of Glory.* New York: HarperCollins, 1976.

Lohrey, Amanda. "The Big Nothing: Lawrence Krauss and Arse-Kicking Physics." *The Monthly*. October 2012. accessed on February 15, 2016. https://www.themonthly.com.au/issue/2012/october/1354074365 /amanda-lohrey/big-nothing.

McEwan, Ian. "End of the World Blues." Accessed on June 15, 2016. http://www.skeptic.ca/End_of_World_Blues.htm.

McGrath, Alister and Joanna Collicutt McGrath. *The Dawkins Delusion: Atheist Fundamentalism and the Denial of the Divine.* Downers Grove, IL. InterVarsity, 2007.

Meyer, Stephen C. *Darwin's Doubt.* New York: HarperCollins, 2013.

Milosz, Czelaw. "The Discreet Charm of Nihilism." *New York Review of Books*. November 19, 1998. Accessed on February 15, 2016. http://www.nybooks.com/articles /1998/11/19/discreet-charm-of-nihilism/.

Minsky, Marvin. *The Society of Mind.* New York: Simon & Schuster, 1986.

Mohler, R. Albert Jr. *Atheism REMIX: A Christian Confronts the New Atheists.* Wheaton, IL: Crossway Books, 2008.

Nietzsche, Friedrich Wilhelm. *The Anti-Christ, Ecce Homo, Twilight of the Idols and Other Writings*, ed. Aaron Ridley and Judith Norman. Cambridge: Cambridge University Press, 2005.

_____. *Twilight of the Idols and the Anti-Christ*. London: Penguin, 2003.

Nagel, Thomas. *Mind and Cosmos: Why the Materialist Neo-Darwinian Conception of Nature Is Almost Certainly False.* Oxford: Oxford University Press, 2012.

_____. *The Last Word.* New York: Oxford University Press, 1997.

Onfray, Michael. *Atheist Manifesto: The Case Against Christianity, Judaism, and Islam.* New York: Arcade Publishing, 2008.

Overbye, Dennis. "Zillions of Universes? Or Did Ours Get Lucky?" October 28, 2003. Accessed on January 22, 2016. http://www.nytimes.com/2003/10/28/science /space/28COSM.html?pagewanted=all.

Pearcey, Nancy. *Finding Truth.* Colorado Springs, CO: David C. Cook, 2015.

Perry, Michael J. "The Morality of Human Rights: A Nonreligious Ground?" *Emory Law Journal,* 54, 2005.

Pinker, Steven. *The Blank Slate: The Modern Denial of Human Nature.* New York: Penguin, 2002.

Plantinga, Alvin. "The Dawkins Confusion." Accessed on April 11, 2015. http://www.christianitytoday.com/bc/2007/002/1.21.html.

Prothero, Stephen. *God is Not the One: The Eight Rival Religions That Run the World.* New York: HarperOne, 2010.

Rahe, Paul. *Republics Ancient and Modern: Classical Republicanism and the American Revolution.* Chapel Hill: University of North Carolina Press, 1992.

Riley, Naomi Schaefer. "A Revelation: Civil Debate Over God's Existence." Accessed June 16, 2016. http://www.wsj.com/articles/SB119214767015956720.

Roth, Ariel. *Origins.* Hagerstown, MD: Herald, 1998.

Russell, Bertrand. "A Free Man's Worship." 1903. Accessed on February 15, 2016. http://www3.nd.edu/~afreddos/courses/264/fmw.htm.

_____. *Science and Religion.* Oxford: Oxford University Press, 1935.

_____. *Why I Am Not a Christian: and other essays on religion and related subjects.* New York: Simon & Schuster, 1957.

"Seeking Christian Interiority: An Interview with Louis Dupre," *Christian Century*, July 16-23, 1997.   Accessed February 16, 2016. https://www.questia.com/magazine   /1G1-19651878/seeking-christian-interiority-an-interview-with-louis.

Sellars, Wilfred. *Science, Perception, and Reality.* Atascadero, CA: Ridgeview, 1991.

Shermer, Michael. *How We Believe: Science, Skepticism, and the Search for God.* New York: Holt Paperbacks, 2000.

Singer, Peter. All Animals Are Equal. Accessed on July 15, 2016. http://spot.colorado.edu/~heathwoo/phil1200,Spr07/singer.pdf.

Slingerland, Edward. *What Science Offers the Humanities: Integrating Body and Culture.* New York: Cambridge University Press, 2008.

"Stephen Hawking's ALS Appears to Have 'almost burnt out', Says Neurologist"   Accessed   April   16,   2015. http://www.sciencerecorder.com   /news/stephen-hawkings-als-appears-to-have-almost-burnt-out-says-neurologist/.

Swinburne, Richard. "Design Defended," *Think. Spring 2004.*

Taunton, Larry Alex. *The Faith of Christopher Hitchens: The Restless Soul of the World's Most Notorious Atheist.* Nashville, TN: Nelson Books, 2016.

Third Way magazine, Vol. 26, No. 5, June 2003.

Turek, Frank. *Stealing from God: Why Atheists Need God to Make Their Case*. Carol Stream, IL: NavPress, 2014.

Vilenkin, Alexander. *Many Worlds in One*. New York: Hill and Wang, 2006.

Wald, George. "Life and Mind in the Universe," in *Cosmos, Bios, Theos*, ed. Henry Margenau and Roy Abraham Varghese. La Salle, IL: Open Court, 1992.

Wilson, David Sloan. *Darwin's Cathedral: Evolution, Religion, and the Nature of Society*. Chicago: University of Chicago Press, 2002.

Wolfe, Alan. *The Transformation of American Religion: How We Actually Live Our Faith*. New York: Free Press, 2003.

Wegner, Daniel. *The Illusion of Conscious Will. Cambridge, MA: Massachusetts Institute of Technology, 2002.*

Weinberg, Steven. *The First Three Minutes*. New York: Basic Books, 1993.

The Westminster Confession of Faith. Accessed January 15, 2016. http://www.opc.org /wcf.html#Chapter_01.

Zacharias, Ravi. *The End of Reason: A Response to the New Atheists*. Grand Rapids, MI: Zondervan, 2008.

_____. "The Religious Affiliation of Military & Political Leader Napoleon Bonaparte. Accessed April 28, 2015. http://www.adherents.com/people/pn/Napoleon.html.

Zaimov, Stoyan. "1 in 4 Americans Don't Believe in God; Lack of Trust in Local Churches Cited as a Reason Why Adults Are Leaving the Faith." Accessed March 26, 2015. http://m.christianpost.com/news/barnas-2015-state-of-atheism-report-finds-one-in-four-americans-dont-believe-god-exists--136327/.